From working class HERO to absolute DISGRACE

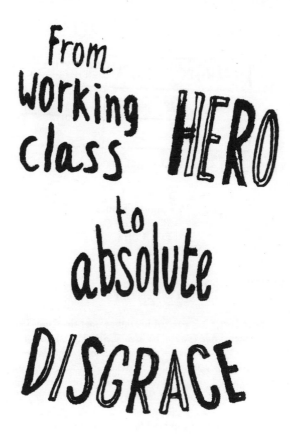

From
Working
class HERO
to
absolute
DISGRACE

STEPHEN FOSTER

First published in 2009 by

Short Books
3A Exmouth House
Pine Street
EC1R 0JH

10 9 8 7 6 5 4 3 2 1

ISBN 978-1-906021-21-4

Printed in Great Britain by Clays, Suffolk
Cover design: Jon Gray

For Bumpy

Preface

It was late at night. I was sitting on a wall dangling a bottle in my hand, looking out over the city. I had just turned forty. I was sitting in a line, in company with several other forty-year- olds. The wall we were on was a school wall. We had been attending an event that could only happen now, in these days, in the new millennium. It could only happen because of the internet, specifically the Friends Reunited website, which allows you to search your old school, add your name to a list, and rediscover old mates, and otherwise. The popularity of this site launched the cult of the class reunion, which, in the case of my generation, coincided with that landmark year during which life begins.

Ours was not the sort of school that would go in for 'old boys' in the normal run of things. It was a 'bog standard' comprehensive, architecturally drab, with an unkempt atmosphere and antique plumbing. Walking the corridors the night of that reunion, I overheard people say things like, 'Look, there's Minnie Caldwell's office, I fucking hated her,' or, 'Look, that was the room where that bastard Westy used to give us the whip.' They were grown up, with children of their own, children who were even attending the same school, but the smells and the lockers and the doorways took them back like it was yesterday, the words they spat out were as fresh and as bitter as the welt from Westy's whip. My feelings were more ambivalent. I had not been whipped often, I had not had a bad time at the place, I had come out of it with seven O levels, two of them grade As. Some pupils did better, but no more than a handful.

I'd heard that the main part of the school was soon to be knocked down and rebuilt. I continued to walk the corridors, running my fingers along the sectional Victorian radiators, like I always used to. I wondered if it might be worth putting in an offer for them, when the demolition started. They'd fetch good money at architectural salvage; you'd have no trouble shifting them where I live now. I'm no longer involved in the building trade, though I was once; it happens, I think, that some small residue of all the things you have been remain a part of you.

I was in a minority at the reunion in the specific sense that I no longer resided in the city, or anywhere near. I'd travelled a couple of hundred miles and from a world away to be there. After a while I began to notice certain obvious absentees, and I asked after them.

'What happened to Macca? Has anybody seen him?'

'Dead,' came the reply.

'Dead? Of what?'

'Drugs.'

'For fuck's sake.'

I considered the fate of Macca, the first amongst us to have had sex with a girl, when he was thirteen. And then I remembered Carter, the class joker. I hadn't spotted him either. How was he doing?

'Dead too.'

'What, drugs again?'

'It was more like drink and drugs in his case, duck.'

'Duck' is the expression of fond address in these parts, duck is as love, or as darling, elsewhere. I must have looked shaken at the news, shaken enough, in any event, for bonny women to pull me to them and hold me safe against their plumptious bosoms. These bonny women were the skinny sirens of our youth, Macca's earlier conquests, Carter's captive audience. I felt happy in their warm embraces, happy and comforted. I could have stayed there a while, which I did. I got slowly drunk, like everybody, until finally I was one of the stragglers left at the end of the night for the sitting-in-a-line-on-the-wall business.

'Look at the city, though, Foster,' one said.

'Doesn't it look beautiful with all the lights twinkling?' another said.

'Yes, it does,' I replied, the only answer I could give, and the true answer too.

'Under cover of darkness, you can't see the burnt-out shopping trolleys,' a third said.

'Or the shopping trolleys up on blocks,' the first said.

They all tipped their cans of bitter and lager and cider to their lips. It had been a bring-your-own do. I lifted my bottle, which was white wine.

'When did you get to become so posh?' the first one said, meaning the wine.

'You're a proper middle-class gayer now, aren't you?' said the second.

They all laughed at this, and at me, which I deserved, having arrived with white wine to such a gathering. What wasn't noted was that it was a Sancerre, a good sauvignon, it had cost over a tenner, though it was a bit tepid now, being the second bottle. The temperature upset me. I didn't mention it.

Middle-class gayer. What a beautiful expression, I thought. And a neologism too, a coinage. We sat there, giggling like schoolboys. The word gayer, I felt sure, was not meant as the mid-mark of a superlative crescendo: gay-gayer-gayest; no, it was rather intended as a sort of job description, as dancer is to dance, as chancer is to chance. And though the homosexual connotation might be implied, they didn't mean it that way, not really. Rather they meant that I had become the sort of fairy who likes poetry and who doesn't have the decency to keep quiet about it, who can probably even recite the stuff. The word made me smile. I was more than content to be described as a gayer: I was delighted. Middle class was a different matter, though. Middle class was where the insult lay. Middle class was something you could say and mean harm by, the words 'middle class' lay a charge against you in this part of the world. Worse, and silently, I conceded that the description was not entirely inaccurate.

I was happy sitting on that wall. I was still down to earth and tough enough to drink my fey tipple straight from the bottle, at least. At least I could say that. But I was on holiday there; I would not be staying to see the burnt-out shopping trolleys in the cold light of day; tomorrow I would be returning to my real life, my life of middle-class gayness.

How is it – how can it be – I thought, as I drove home the following day, that a working-class hero like me had gone to the bad like this?

What follows, more or less, is the answer.

Part One : London calling

I was born and raised in Stoke-on-Trent, the Potteries, as it's known. Natives of Stoke are never far from home; they are reminded of the city whenever they're in a public convenience and see the word Twyfords stamped on the pissoirs and the basins. The acts of urinating and cleaning evoke curious connotations: pissing on, washing your hands of. It used to be the case in a restaurant that I could always spot a fellow Stokie – they were the individuals turning the plate to examine the stamp, to establish that it was proper crockery from Royal Doulton or Wedgwood, not some imposter rubbish from Spain. The practice has all but died out now that we know it will have come from China, but it remained the custom when I stopped turning my own plate in this way, during a period that coincided with my experimenting with my accent, not long after I left Stoke-on-Trent for good. This was a crime I exacerbated by flitting off down south: though Stoke is in the Midlands, it's closer to Manchester than it is to Birmingham, and in any event, on the north/south divide, all of these cities are the north.

In northern working-class culture, jobs, marriages, children and all the rest will partially define you, but if you're looking to create a big impact, leave your home town. Turning your back on your roots is an act that arouses suspicion, is an act that can, and will, be used in evidence against you. Leaving will secure you the opposite of a good character reference.

Not good enough for you round here any more?

This is the accusation, the implication being that you think you're better than this. Leaving is the signifier of a couple more associated personality faults, while we're at it:

One: you think you're someone

and

Two: (it follows on from thinking you're someone): you've become too big for your boots.

The only exception to the rule is if you join the forces, a different matter that can be regarded as a sabbatical from which it is expected that you will return home, one way or another, with honour, having performed a patriotic act, having carried out a duty.

Otherwise, leaving is wrong. You could hang about to argue the toss, but what's the point? Those mouthing the allegations about your opinion of yourself are only kids, the same as you. But they are kids who have already settled for their lot in life. To your way of thinking, they have already settled for less. Still, whatever your philosophical differences on, and at, this moment of departure, there remain many characteristics that you all still have in common. Principal amongst these is chippiness.

So you do bother to argue the toss. You don't think that you're someone, as a matter of fact, and you're not too big for your boots either, by the way, so shut it.

'You'll be back soon enough. With your tail between your legs.'

London Calling

No, you will not be back soon enough. You will not be back soon enough precisely because the place is a dump full of people like them. You may acknowledge that fact quietly to yourself, or you may make an issue of it and start a new argument. It's up to you. Whichever, you have to silently concede the truth of the key allegation: you *are* too good for round here, as a matter of fact, you *are* better than this. You are not yet nineteen; you can be forgiven for thinking only too-true thoughts like that. But at least you have elected to keep quiet about it. You are in enough trouble as it is, without bringing that matter out into the open.

*****

I waited outside Stoke railway station, smoking a cigarette. Across the road stood the city's grand hotel, the North Staffs. I had once worked a few casual shifts there as a waiter, serving the Rotarians and the Law Society their Christmas dinners. Exactly where these bigwigs came from I did not know: I had never seen them walking around my streets. I suspect, now, that this was because they lived in chalets in the bordering county of Cheshire, the 'suburb' of Stoke-on-Trent where those businessmen and professionals who need to work in the city prefer to reside. The North Staffs is one of the few imposing edifices in Stoke, constructed in the Jacobean style. A statue of Josiah Wedgwood stands outside. Wedgwood established several factories in the Potteries, and one district. The district, the world's first industrial village, he called Etruria, in the mistaken belief that Greek vases were Etruscan in origin. The factory at Etruria has gone – it became the world's first post-industrial village too – but the area remains and is still known as Etruria (the Florence of the Midlands). It's a romantic name for a gloomy vale; a romantic name which comes out of an erroneous concept, which is typical of Stoke. The city is commonly referred to as the Five Towns, another 'mistake', this one made by Arnold Bennett in his Clayhanger novels: Bennett apparently thought that 'the Five Towns' was more euphonious than 'the Six Towns', which is the real number. This promiscuity regarding facts and details tends to foster an ethos of make-do-and-mend, change the rules as you go, and if something's slightly wrong (like the naming of Etruria, or the number of the towns), not to worry because, 'It'll do.'

I grew up thinking 'It'll do' was the city motto.

I stubbed my cigarette out and took a last look at Josiah Wedgwood before making my way onto the platform. I had selected my departure outfit carefully. I wore a 'Setting Sons' T-shirt, the cover art of the most recent album by The Jam. The T-shirt image depicted another bronze statue, of three battered war heroes supporting each other against a lowering sky. I too was dressed for battle. I was wearing an Iranian army surplus jacket over the T-shirt. Surplus jackets were à la mode. After many hours spent in the surplus shop considering the matter, I had chosen the jacket for the simplicity of its cut and for the minimalism of the insignia, a plain white star on each lapel, one of which I covered with a CND badge.

Though I was in fatigues, I was not off to war; not so far as I knew, anyway: I was off to a hotel in the Strand. Such anti-southern-ness as I harboured as a consequence of natural osmosis, absorbed via background, did not amount to much. I found the ritual default – the knee-jerk antipathy of northerners to southerners – backward and embarrassing. What I'd seen of London, from a couple of day trips with college, I liked, a lot. I liked the shops, I liked the tube and the traffic, I liked the extraordinary foodstuffs and emporia, I liked the clothes, and I liked the girls with their fantastically snooty attitudes. I liked the pace. I found it slightly frightening, as all of us did, if we were honest, but I was seduced by it too. And though I joined my peers in mocking 'Cockney' pronunciation, in truth I even liked the way they talked and the words they used. This, after all, was the same lingo that my heroes, The Jam, and my other heroes, The Clash, used. These two great groups had followed in the footsteps of the trailblazing great group, the Sex Pistols. All three of these bands were from London or thereabouts, so I adopted the opposite stance to anti-southern-ness, not just as a matter of teenage perversity, but because I believed that the south, or London, at any rate, was better than Stoke. I could not say that out loud, of course, because it would be more than wrong, it would be a heresy to speak against my own tribe in such a way.

'I'll tell thee the only good thing about London – the road out of it!'

This was the most common line people used when conversation about the capital city arose.

'You never see a bloody white face down there!'

This was the second-most common line people came out with.

In my eyes anti-southern-ness went beyond nonsense; it also invoked the sort of normal, everyday racism that is not only typical of Stoke but typical of England. To a certain sort of young white guy, racism is just about the worst thing in the world; I was that certain sort of young white guy.

On the other hand, though, there was no denying that aside from all the promise that attracted me to 'the Smoke' – the 'groovy' alternative name these London-haters sometimes used (which puzzled me, because Stoke beat London hands down when it came to smokiness) – it was, all the same, the seat and powerbase of the Conservative government. The Tories were determined to denude the north by destroying its strength: organised labour. I knew this, because everybody told me as much, and I hated the Tories at least as much as I hated racists.

So, even if Stoke was populated by a number of regional

separatists, certain aspects of the city (and by extension, both the north and the Midlands) encapsulated an idea and an ideal that I would always be obliged to defend. That ideal was social equality. Achieving social equality required an inversion of the existing status quo: it required a revolution. I might have been on the move geographically, but politically I remained in the same place. I knew on which side of the line I stood. It was Us (working-class heroes) against Them (all classes who were not working-class heroes). If you grew up in a manufacturing city in the seventies, it was your birthright to own a secure sense of self like this. The most vibrant expression of community that came about through this sense of collective identity was found in industrial confrontation. To me a good strike with a picket line, barking dogs, scabs being bussed in, coppers in riot gear and crowd surges, ending up with an all-out scrap, was an event that rivalled a football match. And it was free, too.

It's not like Stoke everywhere. Over the years I have heard people come out with this sort of talk:

I come from X, originally – the place means nothing to me, I feel no affinity with it, I never felt like I belonged there, to be honest, not really. I don't even think of it as home now, no; it never crosses my mind.

When you ask, X turns out to be Nuneaton, Daventry, Northampton, even Coventry, where they at least made Rolls Royce engines, though as George Orwell says in *The Road to Wigan Pier*, 'in Coventry, you might as well be in Finsbury Park'. X is never Sheffield, Manchester, Liverpool or Leeds. X is never a dirty, big city with a dirty, big beating heart, where local politics are red in tooth and claw, talked about on buses and in market places, and important. Out of forty or so representatives sitting on Stoke council you could count a grand total of zero Conservatives. I often heard it said that a monkey could be elected in the Potteries so long as it stood on a Labour ticket. It wasn't so much what you were *for* that mattered, it was what you were *against*. You were against the shiftless capitalist bastards of the boss class down south who held all the aces of birth and privilege, who pissed away the hard graft of your 'brothers' by gambling with it in that wide boy's casino, the Stock Exchange.

My outlook was shaped by coming of age in this climate, in a time and a place that consisted of the fraught years immediately prior to the transition: the death of manufacturing industry and the birth of service.co.uk, the world of today, the land of off-shore call centres and Chinese illegals drowning in Morecambe Bay. To make way for this improvement, the traditional working classes had to be phased out. We might win the odd battle, but we were certainly losing the war. Every week there were more lay-offs and more redundancies as the condition of mass unemployment that the Tories had deliberately created – as part of their campaign of hatred against us – began to bite. This produced a situation which made leaving home that much more obvious, of course, yet equally that much more philosophically awkward: while it was more pragmatic to leave, it was at the same time more treacherous. Wasn't it my duty to stay and fight? Not really, not in my line of business.

I had trained to become a chef. Even in France, with its dual narrative of haute cuisine and revolution, chefs are not much associated, either in fact or in the public mind, with the call to arms. In an England of potted-meat paste, margarine and Smash instant potato, where the nation's idea of a culinary delight involved consuming a pancake filled with tinned cherry pie filling at a Little Chef roadside café, all the more the less so.

In choosing a vocational course after leaving school, I had fol-lowed one of my principal interests: cooking. It was a calling that led me into the type of workplaces that were as far removed from mass industry as it's possible to find. Catering workers operate in small units of low-wage, non-union-represented groups, a state of affairs I resented. But I could not say I did not enjoy my work, because I did: I loved it.

My initial attraction to the stove was a matter of necessity. I had a mother who was well ahead of her time; like Carrie in *Sex and the City*, the only thing she ever successfully made in the kitchen was a mess. And several small fires. A disciple of convenience food, she counted the aforementioned Smash along with Findus Crispy Pancakes and dried Vesta Curries amongst the great inventions of the twentieth century. Smash came in small rough granules designed to be rehydrated with boiling water in order to form 'potato.' The granules could also be taken in their neat form, a discovery made by my younger brother, Bumble, whose real name is Andrew, but who wanted a nickname (and Sting had already gone). Bumble used to mainline Smash granules as a snack, downing them in handfuls, like peanuts. I would look at him and imagine, indeed hope, that one day he would overdose, that his stomach would blow up in the kinetic energy of duodenal indigestion. Though he was a very accident-prone boy who could not encounter a lamppost without running into it, and who later survived a fall from a six-storey building, he never did explode.

As the eldest child of three (there is our younger sister, Diane, three years behind Bumble, who was three years behind me), and in the service of our family diet, as well as a function of personal disposition, it was me who stepped into the culinary void that my mother's laissez-faire attitude had created. Even before we acquired Henry, a Spanish waiter stepfather, a maître d' (when I was twelve), I was often to be found experimenting with dishes from magazines, or from my great auntie Mary's collection of Hamlyn Step-by-Step cookery cards. Later, I copied recipes from *Carrier's Kitchen*, a programme hosted by the pioneering television chef, Robert Carrier. Carrier was a fey, drawly American whose show was on in the afternoon. I would catch it when I was skiving school, or revising, as it was known. He was especially influenced by Moroccan cuisine, and was a lover of offal. I remember watching as he made a fan of avocado pear and then interwove the leaves of the fan with slices of pan-fried *foie de veau*.

'Or,' he advised, 'you can substitute lamb's liver, if you can't get *foie de veau*.'

It looked beautiful. It was something I had to try. There was a traditional Victorian market hall a mile from where we lived, with a whole aisle of stalls where fat butchers flashed cleavers against sharpening steels while flirting with housewives. Offal was inexpensive; they practically gave the stuff away with the lights (the lamb's lungs, hanging from a branch of trachea) for the cat. You could forget enquiring after *foie de veau* down here, unless you wanted to find yourself the subject of a Bateman cartoon: The Boy Who Asked For Calves' Liver in Tunstall Market!

Neither could you find an avocado on the greengrocer stalls, not for any money. It wasn't until the first Asian corner shop opened that I was able to buy one of those; I once saw a girl scream when she caught sight of an aubergine in amongst the more identifiable fruit and vegetables in their display. So instead I made Devilled Kidneys. A dozen kidneys cost little more than a packet of biscuits. You could put together ingredients for Devilled Kidneys en Croute and still have enough change from a pound for ten Player's No. 6, the basic cigarette. There was usually Harvey's Bristol Cream to be found in the sideboard, for the devilling. The sideboard was seldom used except to rest your backside against. It had pull-down doors which concealed velvet and mirrored compartments containing half-used bottles of Advocaat, and obscure sundries such as Angostura Bitters. Apart from use in cooking, the sherry only came out at Christmas, when Auntie Mildred, who led the choir at the Methodist chapel, and Uncle Eric, who smoked a pipe and had a beautiful train-sweeper moustache, paid their annual festive visit.

Neither my brother nor sister cared for Devilled Kidneys much, that was the only thing. They would pull faces and spit it out onto the side of the plate. Later in the evening they could be found compensating for the traumatic experience by making 'Cheese'. Cheese was our mother's signature dish, notable for its simplicity and economy of effort.

Recipe for Cheese:
Arrange slices of cheddar to cover a dinner plate.
Flood the plate with milk to within an inch of the lip,
and stick under a hot grill until it bubbles brown.
Remove.
Allow to cool for a minute or two.

To serve:
Accompany with tomato ketchup or brown sauce, or both, and many slices of bread and butter for mopping up. *White* bread and butter, not that brown stuff your big brother has bought home for his repulsive idea of making a tomato sandwich.
Cheese is excellent comfort food, ideal for filling a gap after you've been used as a guinea pig for some idiot notion of cuisine.

*****

The arrival of the Spanish maître d' came as a consequence of divorce, of which there was an epidemic. The first boy amongst us whose parents separated sat next to me in class. It was 1972; we were ten-year-olds. There was none of the culture of counselling which has since been imposed by generations of do-gooders. The culture of counselling is the sort of thing that irritates the fuck out of me now, and would turn me into a grumpy old man, were it not for the fact that programmes on the BBC featuring media-type grumpy old men being grumpy irritate me even more. At least they serve as a compelling warning against the condition: if middle-aged middle-class males weren't so slyly vain and obviously arrogant, they might be better equipped to see that this brand of television is worse than just about anything they can find to moan about, up to and including the culture of counselling. When a boy in our school fell off his bike one day on his way home, cracked his head, went into a coma for three weeks and subsequently died, we did not have counselling for it; we had an assembly with a moment's silence, which left us with the memory of him and the realisation that life, and death, are random, so watch out (for all the good it'll do you).

In place of the culture of counselling there was an ad hoc arrangement called normal human kindness. The first boy whose parents separated was occasionally taken aside and spoken to nicely by teachers, who would sometimes supplement the nice talk with milk, biscuits and sweets. The rest of us were envious of his treatment, and perhaps that boy started a craze, because by the time my cohort had finished school six years later, more than half of us could boast that we came from a 'broken home'. Research on the exploding divorce rate around the early seventies suggests that increased disposable income amongst the working classes might provide a partial explanation for the phenomenon. Between the wars, for instance, 90,000 people sought a divorce but were unable to obtain one because of their inability to meet the likely legal costs. Added to this, we were living in the post-sixties world: that decade's manifesto of satisfaction through personal fulfilment was filtering down and translating itself into real behaviour amongst practising mums and dads even in the dark corners of northern England. Soon enough, the single Latin expression with which schoolchildren were all familiar was *decree nisi*.

I knew little about the way in which the divorces of my class-mates' parents were conducted, however. Commonplace as the business of 'splitting up' had become, it was a subject that remained taboo insofar as talking about it amongst ourselves was concerned. 'Always arguing' was about as much information as anyone was prepared to offer. My own parents wrote 'living separate lives' on the paperwork that led to their decree nisi. I knew this, because my mum told me everything: I was her confessor. Separate lives meant, for a time, that our father, on returning home from work, developed a rather artificial routine whereby he cooked his own Findus Crispy Pancakes for his dinner. But after he had moved out (taking 'separate lives' to its logical conclusion), scenes involving a newly installed lodger, a red sports car, the maître d', the return appearance of our father and an episode of fisticuffs on the front hardstanding told a slightly different story, and told it to the world at large while it was at it. Though the narrative was difficult to follow, I was disgusted at having our dirty laundry aired in this way, even if I knew what was coming by virtue of mother's preview whisperings. I am inherently inhibited – the worst thing that happened to me at school was being made to perform in a play. This characteristic means that, at one level at least, I have always had the potential to become a member of the middle classes: the novelist Sándor Márai says of his bourgeois Hungarian middle-class upbringing, 'By the time I was ten years old I was as self-conscious and quiet, as attentive and well behaved, as the president of a major bank.' That was me, except that in Stoke-on-Trent nobody is all that well behaved. Still, I remain uncomfortable when put into a position where I might be subject to scrutiny by the wider public – with the exception of writing, of course. But writing is invisible as an act, and writing helps with inhibition and with most other things too: writing allows you to edit the world so that it can at least be made to read well, whatever happened.

London Calling

So, as a consequence of my disposition, I was unhappy with those scenes on the front hardstanding. Adult fighting is frightening, close up; I was unhappy about that too. And then I was unhappy for the obvious further reason: behind the net curtains across the road there was an audience of fascinated gawpers lapping up every minute of the sideshow. In short, I was unhappy in triplicate.

Those houses on the other side of the street were small Victorian terraces. On our side we lived in thirties semis with a drive at the side and a garage at the end. The view from our bedroom window at the back of the house gave onto a parallel avenue of more semis; beyond them you could look north to good council houses or south to a bad estate. Most of the geography of Stoke is laid out in this way, with close proximity between the various kinds of housing stock. Broadly speaking, all of the residents of these homes were working class, but there were many distinctions within that category: clean or unclean; free school meals or paid for; car owner or bus; private or rented; good or bad council. Good and bad council could coexist on opposite sides of the same road, or even closer than that. My granny on my father's side used to refer to Mrs Reardon Next Door as 'that common woman', because Mrs Reardon Next Door hung her washing out in her front garden and occasionally marched out in her apron to bellow down the street. Good council looks down on bad council; bad council couldn't care less. It's a truism that the further to the political left you go, the nearer you come to completing the circle and meeting the far right – and so it goes for class. In my experience, top-end upper and bottom-rung lower have a great deal in common: neither gives a stray fart what anyone thinks about them, both love gambling and fighting and are hard as nails (the outdoor swimming pool at Eton is the second-coldest water I have ever entered), and each group has exceptionally poor personal hygiene (posh girls' knickers do not stand up to close scrutiny). Additionally, you could sit them all around the table together and they would accept whatever there was on offer in terms of booze, drugs, or grub without question or complaint. Boris Johnson, the old Etonian Conservative MP and mayor of London, in a questionnaire in *Waitrose Food Monthly* magazine answers the question, 'Are you a fussy eater?' as follows:

'Definitely not; I consider all food to be delicious.'

You could give Boris Johnson a turnip sandwich and he would say thank you. For the toff class, as for the lower working class, food is fodder and always welcome, though the motives for the unified responses do differ. Whereas those at the bottom may not know where the next meal is coming from, toffs pay no attention to what is on their plate for fear that to consider the matter at all would be to put themselves on a par with the serving classes.

So far as the middle classes are concerned, it is in Jamie Oliver's Sainsbury's, rather than in John Lewis's Waitrose that you will find them shopping for food. Though Waitrose might suit them better in terms of its range, it is overpriced, and they do not like wasting money. I bumped into a dean of studies from the University of East Anglia (where I was doing a bit of tutoring) in my local Waitrose. He smiled a guilty smile as we caught sight of each other. It was as if I'd caught him eyeing up a Range Rover in a four-by-four showroom. He was quick to exonerate his presence in the upmarket supermarket in our small talk:

'It's *space* we're really buying, isn't it, Stephen?' he said, casting his eyes around the sparsely populated aisles.

It's a neat trick, turning the matter semiotic, and an illustrative line too: note the use of 'we're'. In employing it, the academic ensures that I become collusive in his choice of grocer. *We* is a big word for the middle class. When a mother in Waitrose says, 'We don't have that now, do we?' as little Daisy reaches for something sweet, pink and forbidden, it has the same effect as a clip round the ear over at Asda. Middle-class codes are verbal, not physical;

language is the agent of control and *we* is the key. It means everything and nothing all at the same time. At a certain point in my life I attended a few PTA meetings at my son Jack's first school, which was situated in a leafy avenue in Norwich where *we* were all really, really socially concerned and committed lovely people, except for me. I was pretty certain that I didn't agree with any tacit agreement of who *we* were; there was no way I was going to be belonging to a group of individuals who were into World Music, who drove derelict 2CVs, whose hair featured two stray plaited dreadlocks with beads threaded on, and whose children took lessons in freeform dance and were *gifted*. Less than no connection, I felt positively antithetical to my co-parents, who clearly considered themselves to be *nice*. I've have always been suspicious of nice people. They are not working-class heroes, and they must have something to hide. But on the other hand, I would never in a million years have taken Jack back to Stoke to be educated amongst the burnt-out shopping trolleys up on blocks. Here is the defining characteristic of the middle-class arriviste: you are a misfit. Like Joey in the Bob Dylan song of the same name, you are always on the outside of whatever side there is.

*****

My maternal grandparents both died when Mother was young, leaving her an only child and an orphan. She was 'passed around the relatives' until she came of age, at which point she made the reasonable decision to run away to work on the funfair in the north Wales holiday resort of Rhyl. Mother's parents had been neither good nor bad council, they were considerably more upmarket than that – my grandfather died on a tennis court, which, though I'd never seen him, created a certain image in my mind of a man from an old black and white movie, wearing flannels and smoking a cigar. One consequence of these circumstances was that a financial arrangement had been put in place that meant that Mother came into a small inheritance upon marriage. With this in mind she agreed to the first acceptable man who proposed; together with my father she was able to buy a two-bed terraced house just as soon as the marriage licence was signed. The inheritance of £500 was enough to purchase the place outright. It was big enough for four of us, but when Diane came along an extra bedroom was required; the terrace was sold in order to upgrade to the semi.

Not all families could afford this: I had plenty of friends who slept three to a bedroom, though the sexes were always segregated. Diane was born with a hole in her heart and had to have two major operations at the special heart unit at Birmingham to survive. This involved a great deal of worry, of course, and I was tearful when she came home after the second operation, the major one, when she was three. I saw the long scar and stitches down her front where the sternum had been split. It was heavily bruised. It seemed cruel, and violent, an awful thing to do to such a small child, and a girl at that, and my sister to boot. I could have killed them for it. However, boys will be boys and it was not all that long before it was business as usual and Bumble and I were tormenting her in our established pre-op way. She is a redhead and has the temper to go with it: it was one of our joys to provoke her into a rage just so we could watch her fly up the stairs like a rocket and slam her bedroom door so hard that the windows rattled while she shouted that she hated us and hoped we would die. This rowdiness was something for our new neighbours to frown down at. The initial inheritance and the subsequent profit on the first house meant that we were living slightly above our station in the thirties semi, a fact of which I was aware. One evening before contracts were exchanged, I had taken a friend up to High Lane – a deceptively bucolic name for a main road – to show him the place that was to be our new home. I was seven or eight. In the way of a seven- or eight-year-old, I knocked on the door and introduced myself to the sellers. They were a stuffy middle-aged couple who were not quite able to stifle their faint sense of horror at being confronted by a couple of young boys out unsupervised *at that time of night*.

That wasn't really on, not back then.

Some of the neighbours, as it turned out, were from the professional classes – one couple were teachers. My father was a painter and decorator who worked for a firm that carried out industrial contracts on new housing developments or road bridges. At night, after tea, he went back to work, to decorate the houses of private individuals, for extra money. 'Off out on a foreigner', as it was known. Around the time that my parents started living separate lives, my mother took up work too. Her first job was collecting football coupons for Littlewoods on a Friday night. This led on to full-time work in credit drapery. Credit drapery entailed selling household goods – tea towels, pots and pans, Mouli-graters and other kitchen gadgets – from the back of a Mini van around council estates. The Mini van was a company car and was the main incentive in taking the job. It gave my mother access to wheels; in her words, it gave her freedom. She later graduated from credit drapery to running a book. Running a book involves loaning cash for money-lending firms: loan sharks, as they are known in the popular imagination, or social workers, as my mother tended to see them; social workers, only useful ones – able to provide a helpful hundred quid to pay off the gas bill along with a bit of tea and sympathy. Running a book was a job that included an upgrade on the Mini van. Mother could now be seen out and about in a Ford saloon. Small wonder they could afford to supply better cars, the interest they charged.

'These families have no current accounts, duck, the banks won't have them, not with their track records, that's what you don't understand; it's only the same as an overdraft for people with money.'

This was the response she gave when I made pointed remarks regarding the matter of her acting for a firm who lent at an annual rate that worked out at twelve hundred per cent. I had joined the Labour Party at fourteen, and attended a couple of meetings too, in a room above the working men's club. I was a socialist, an activist, a Man of the People. I had a selection of political sticks with which to beat her, but she was my mum, so I let her off most of the time. And anyway, she had her way of dealing with any perceived criticism. Her response to the sideshow on our hardstanding was typical: to my look of disapprobation regarding the fisticuffs she simply said, 'It'll give them something to talk about,' meaning the nosey parkers across the road. And then she'd spark up another Consulate to 'calm her nerves'.

They were up there with Smash, the new menthol cigarettes. 'Cool as a mountain spring,' said the advertising slogan. They must have had excellent health-giving properties, because the games master at school smoked them too. I took one from Mother to try out. It was like inhaling toothpaste, one of the worst ideas ever conceived. A rumour going around at the time was that if you baked a banana skin in the oven, then scraped down the dried inner peel and rolled it up and smoked it, you would get stoned. You didn't – there was absolutely no high involved – it just tasted foul and made you cough and gag, but in my view, it was a happier experience than cooling out with a Consulate.

After the dust had settled on the divorce, Henry the maître d' moved in full time. First things first, our family was moved to a 'pleasure gardens' on the Isle of Man for a year. The pleasure gardens were an enterprise based on the attraction to holidaymakers of a number of small fragments of a ruined abbey plus a field of strawberry beds. Mother and Henry were managing the place for a friend of Henry's in order to 'get away from everything' for a while. We went there in a moonlight flit. During the school summer holidays I worked twelve hours a day in the cafeteria. I was thirteen years old; it was my full kitchen apprenticeship. The steam ran out on the Isle of Man adventure (the business was possibly collapsing) and we were back in Stoke within a year. The gossip about us from the nosey parkers across the road had been tremendous, I learned. We had emigrated to America, Australia; Henry was dead, all sorts.

I returned to my previous school, told the deputy head what O levels I had been doing in the Isle of Man, and was put into the top form – G – which stood for Grammar. The next stream down, S, stood for Secondary, and it was here that the majority of my erstwhile mates were to be found. S is where I would have chosen to go (to stay with them) had I have been there at the time when the choices were made rather than in the Isle of Man serving up cottage pie and chips. After G and S the streaming was A,B,C,D. Those in A took a few CSEs; those in B,C and D took no exams at all; they were 'factory fodder'.

I did not want to be in with the swots. I tried changing down to S, but they would not let me drop three O level subjects, which was what it amounted to. It was an iniquitous situation. First I had been removed from the school, and now that I was back I had been displaced again. I was an exile in my own land. An exile with a dago wop for a stepfather. One or two thickheads mentioned this. Bumble, who was only in the first year, was an excellent fighter, the best in the school. A word with him would usually see the thickheads sorted out, and I could kick them myself in the melée of the scrap, once they were down on the deck.

Henry had changed his name from the original Enrique because none of the English were able to pronounce it. I would not tell Henry that he was causing me trouble (by being a dago wop), but he could see that there was something up, that I was a little listless. His diagnosis was that I was not doing enough on

33

the extra-curricular side, that I was missing my twelve-hour shifts in the cafeteria. He did his bit to help: soon enough he was finding me work in the restaurants in which he was employed. These changed frequently, the way of life in catering. The establishments were country pubs with restaurants attached. They were located in south Cheshire where the Rotarians lived, or else on the fringes of the Peak District in neighbouring Derbyshire. Here the clientele consisted of fat men toting cigars, accompanied by their wives and fancy bits. The wives and fancy bits formed an identical chorus wrapped in halos of peroxide, wrists jangling with gold charms and pendants on chains disappearing deep into mesmerising valleys of tanned and wrinkled décolletage. There were no posh places like this in Stoke. The only exotic restaurants of which we were aware were the new wave of Chinese and Indian. Otherwise, it was a Berni Steakhouse or a Wimpy. There seemed to be no employment laws out in the hills of Derbyshire or along the plains of Cheshire, though, and I liked that. I was collecting glasses and pulling pints at the age of fourteen, and being paid cash-in-pocket for my troubles.

Henry was five-foot-nothing and a 'character', with a character's line in patter. He was in the right sort of work – the maître d' runs front of house, and front of house is 'on the boards' in restaurant terms. I don't like characters, they annoy me. But I always needed money for something, so I put up with working alongside him until one day I got my big break: I was tapped up by a head chef. Backstage was where the real talent hung out, backstage was where the art took place; everybody knew that. Even in the late seventies, before it was commonplace for chefs to consider themselves first and foremost celebrities, they were a breed that came equipped with overblown superiority complexes: any tool can carry plates and glasses back and forth, whereas a chef's work is skilled, demanding, dangerous, specialised and unique – the establishment is nothing without him. *Nothing.* And to a degree, chefs were correct in this assessment of their place in the grand scheme of things. You would occasionally overhear people make a remark like, 'We don't go to the Old Vicarage any more, we've defected over to the Feathers – *no one* does a Bœuf Wellington like Michel.'

The fact was that the restaurant traded on Michel's reputation. But even though he knew as much, and would indeed encourage trade to follow him when he moved, it took a further decade and the introduction of a fully operational market economy for the floodgates to truly open: for Raymond, Anton, Marco and all the rest to begin to apply this truth and to start opening restaurants and franchises in their own names. It took market capitalism for chefs to become free, free to keep their own hard-earned profits and not have to hand it over to Mr Big, who sat at the bar all night drinking Chivas Regal in the company of peroxide wife No. 3, the champion of champions when it came to décolletage: the deepest, the wrinkliest, and accessorised with the most gold. This impending triumph of market capitalism was a difficult socio-political contradiction for me to absorb, because although I was effectively a Marxist thinker, of course, like all chefs, I wanted to be free too.

Outside of the serious and intense activity that comprises the two-hour heat of service, chefs devote what remains of their energy to screwing. Anything left over after that is dedicated to belittling and playing practical jokes on the waiting staff. The two worker groups rely on each other for their living, but their relationship is wholly dysfunctional, a state of affairs that threw Henry and I into an awkward situation. My new stepfather was now from the wrong side of the tracks twice over: not only was he a Johnny Foreigner, he was also a fucking waiter.

Henry had been resident in the UK for a good number of years, having fled General Franco's persecution of Barcelonians such as himself at some indeterminate point in history – the

copy of the Sex Pistol's *Never Mind the Bollocks*, smashing the vinyl into pieces, not just because my brother played it too loud and too often, but because it was an unacceptable foul *noise*, it was not proper music, beautiful and moving, like *Carmen* and all the other crappy operas he insisted on inflicting on us while once again dabbing at his teary eye with the corner of his mono-grammed handkerchief.

That we all managed to rub along reasonably well for the most part was a testament to the best of him, particularly his way with a homespun Catalunyan homily: 'Stephens,' he would say (he never, ever, got my name right, always referring to me in the plural), 'Stephens, always remember this: the prick is a very short, but the life is a very long.'

'Okay.'

'So, Stephens?' he would ask, raising an eyebrow, waiting for an answer, seeking reassurance that he had been understood.

'So be careful what I do with my a prick?'

'And?'

'And where I put it?'

'Correct – and where you *put it*,' he would say, sternly, yet triumphantly, giving a stern yet triumphant clap of his hands.

I might have been a sarcastic boy who colluded in chef-led mockery of him and his kind, I might not have spoken Cata-lunyan all that a perfect, but at least I had followed him on this crucial point.

I tried to imagine a short prick juxtaposed with a long life, an awkward image to call to mind, but an idea to make me laugh out loud, the more so when I encouraged Henry to repeat the line to my friends, who were tickled pink, and with whom it counted well, neutralising his dago-wopness a great deal, and turning him into something of a cult hero.

Beyond his homilies, there were his ways. When he first caught me smoking at the age of fourteen, he said, 'Stephens, don't do that behind my a back. Be a man about it and do it in the open.'

From that point on he used to toss me a pack of twenty Benson & Hedges – Catch – every Thursday from the carton of two hundred that he purchased from the Co-Op. They were decent, too, Bensons, superior to Player's No. 6, no question. This act of misjudged generosity (Lung cancer? *Qué?*) left him with a couple of day's supply for himself. His smoking habits were Continental: he always had a cigarette on the go, and would often forget where he stood, so that he had one in his mouth, one in his hand and another smouldering away in an ashtray. He was a dedicated sixty-a-day man. He also stirred three sugars into the many, many cups of Nescafé that sustained him – he drank three mugs of coffee (nine sugars), each accompanied by a B&H, in bed in the morning before he had even got his pants on. Otherwise, he existed more or less entirely on biscuits and Catalunyan Bread, a speciality of his homeland. In time, we came to understand the distinction between the Catalan and the Spaniard.

'In Seville they grow oranges, in Barcelona we turn them into marmalade and make money out of them,' he would say. 'That's why they hate us.'

In retrospect I can easily see why he was such a chippy irritant: in UK terms he was a short-arsed Welshman with a regional persecution/superiority complex.

Catalunyan Bread is not a loaf of Mother's Pride. It's a French stick split in half, drizzled with olive oil (not Trex), rubbed with cut garlic, and smeared with the pips and juice of fresh tomatoes. Catalunyan Bread is a tapas staple, one that benefits from being left to stand for an hour for the flavours to blend. It's an uncommon snack in High Lane, Stoke-on-Trent, but one for which we, and certain of our friends, acquired a taste. Henry would occasionally supplement this basic diet with a tin of sardines. Once, after a particularly gruelling weekend of double shifts, I saw him eat two T-bone steaks in succession, but that was a one-off and caused trouble. 'Fuck me a Stephens,' he said, 'I cannot fucking shit.'

So far as drink was concerned, you might find him with a whisky and Coke in his hand at any time of day or night, and it was not possible to eat biscuits, Catalunyan Bread, or sardines, without the accompaniment of a glass of wine. Anything would do, duty-free plonk at five francs a litre from the campsite shop was just as acceptable as a Rioja Gran Reserva. Between cigarettes he occasionally opened his box of Montecristo cigars and sniffed at the contents. Some of the cigars came in metal tubes which Bumble would steal for keeping maggots, for fishing, a crime he would always deny. The Montecristo box also contained a device for snipping a cigar-tip in order to ventilate it correctly for the perfect smoke. On feast days and Sunday evenings Henry would press this tool into service. He lit his cigar with dedicated cigar-lighting matches, which were brown and friable, like charcoal, to distinguish the ceremony from the everyday sparking of a Benson. Some of the cigars were ten inches long; relishing one was an activity that lasted about three hours and saw him disappear into, and under, a cloud of fug.

I had no wish to know anything about the length of his prick, but the way he carried on, if it was to be related to the likely length of his life, I reckoned it would be very short indeed.

*****

My girlfriend refused to come to see me off to London. We were in a steady relationship. We had been going out for over two years, since before my final school exams (she was one school year younger). If I was betraying my home and everything it stood for by leaving Stoke-on-Trent, this was nothing compared to what I was doing to Jacqui. The idea of watching me depart was too painful, though she was going to write every day. So I boarded the train to Euston alone, equipped with my weekly ration of fags and a copy of the *NME*. I was on my way to the interview; I hadn't even got the job yet.

My fellow travellers played cards and grumbled. Some got quietly, or noisily, drunk, and most smoked: the sectioned-off carriages towards the rear of the train were set aside for that minority interest, non-smoking. The reading matter spread about the tables consisted of the *Mirror*, the *Sun* and the odd *Daily Express*, a paper that was still run off as a broadsheet. The *Express* would soon shed the upmarket pretensions that went with its size and would also downgrade to a tabloid. I don't think I had ever seen anyone with a copy of the *Daily Mail* (the paper of choice for both my parents now), and I'd only once seen a beardy on the bus with his head in the *Guardian*. Nobody I knew read a broadsheet, a 'quality', as they were known, because those papers reported different lives and spoke in an alien register, though in my latter days at college I would pick up a *Guardian* myself sometimes, as a pose, which can only mean that the beardy had in some way impressed me. I began reading *The Times* when I found myself settled into room service at the Savoy; I had heard somewhere about the extraordinary length of Bernard Levin's sentences, so I started by looking for those.

Along with journalists from the *NME* – writers like Paul Morley and Ian Penman who were working in fantastical lexicons of their own paradigm – broadsheet journalists, especially those notable names from the back pages – Brian Glanville and Hugh McIlvanney – became important people to me. Work in room service usually afforded a decent amount of time for idling, time I devoted to drinking beer while reading the papers that the hotel clients left behind. I had always taken refuge in reading: Enid Blyton, *Beano* and *Beezer* comics, my mother's Catherine Cooksons and Isaac Asimovs, *Watership Down* (big in the Isle of

Man), *Smash Hits* and then the *NME*. My reading was catholic and sometimes it taught me things I really ought to have already known. I remember reading Frederick Forsyth's *The Odessa File* long into the small hours when I was fifteen, and having to turn repeatedly to the back jacket to reinform myself that the events contained within were based on truth. How you could get to this age and never have heard of the Holocaust, I don't know. Only in Stoke, as they say. I dropped History at O level: we hadn't had any Holocaust up until that point; when I quit we were on the feudal system, a subject matter that was impossible to stay awake to. I dropped History because I didn't like the master, who was one of the hardliners of the place. We had no uniform, but the school was run in an efficient manner by an elite group of males who specialised in dishing out old-style discipline; the whip, in multiples of three lashes, was the punishment for certain misdemeanours. Brother Bumble used to be sent down for it every day; it was part of his identity. Being beaten was not the deterrent for him that it was for the rest of us. On the contrary, for a heroic person who traded on notoriety, the whip was an essential element in the creation of his own Bumble mythology.

I enjoyed being whipped about as much as I enjoyed the literary syllabus. I took only a partial interest in Eng Lit due to the fact that far too much of the material set before us was written in a dreary, archaic language and featured a ludicrous and implausible plot. The only fun I can ever remember in English was when the master, who was involved in Amateur Dramatics, read aloud from *King Solomon's Mines* last thing on a Friday, as a sort of soapy-serial send-off into the weekend. This master was, like Henry, another short-arse, and rotund with it. He was not one of the whippers; he was more the great toucher-up of girls' bottoms, an activity that many of our female classmates would report to us boys as 'a laugh'. The thespian pervert put on a 'native' accent when reading the parts of Umbopa and the other Kaffirs.

We weren't shocked by this, after all, we lived in a culture where comedians traded on doing 'funny' foreign accents, and in which the sitcom *Love Thy Neighbour* frequently used the words sambo and honky. Rather than consider matters of political correctness (which was not yet invented), we were impressed that he dared risk a performance in front of us at all. It was brave, and in fact he got away with it; he was pretty good and had a twinkle in his eye. I imagine that was how he got away with his gropings too.

In our latter school days, heading towards our final exams, our form tutor set a box at the front of our form room which contained books meant for casual reading during registration and free periods. The most popular title here was Stan Barstow's *A Kind of Loving*. It had a dedicated following, its popularity deriving from the fact that it contained sex scenes, a detail of which the tutor, who could be seen playing in the Salvation Army band at weekends, must surely have been ignorant. But beyond this sensational and subversive attribute, *A Kind of Loving* was set in the contemporary north, and was written in a key that wasn't so far off our own. *A Kind of Loving* painted a world that was recognisable to us, similar to the one we went home to. There were other books like this: *The Loneliness of the Long Distance Runner* by Alan Sillitoe and *A Kestrel for a Knave* by Barry Hines, which we had seen on television as the film *Kes*. These books gave food for thought to a certain type of boy, because they were not written in a dull, antiquated language and did not feature a ludicrous and implausible plot; instead, they introduced the idea that even though music, cars and the opposite sex were the matters of most pressing importance now, if you only knew where to look, there were actually such things as proper books, books that were not written by William Fucking Shakespeare. Also, you also knew that having a Penguin paperback in your pocket would do you no harm in the romancing of a certain kind of girl.

London Calling

*****

I selected a reverse-facing seat amongst the spread of tabloids and *Daily Expresses* as the train pulled away and I watched my old world recede. The 'Evil Bitch' Thatcher was a year into her reign, John Lennon was still alive, the first Mini Metro, the car with which the late Princess of Wales was originally associated, had yet to roll off the assembly lines, as Diana Spencer herself was yet to enter the public consciousness. John McEnroe ruled the world at tennis (even if he had just been defeated by Björn Borg in the famous 18-16 tie-break final). I played a lot of park tennis, though I was never much good. McEnroe was a hero to me, as much for his spectacular disrespect of authority as for his sporting gift. Arthur Scargill, leader of the National Union of Mineworkers, was another like McEnroe, a redhead in a permanent bad mood. Scargill was scowling out of the front page of the *Express* as the train rolled down the track. I was on the same side as him, for sure, though I would never in a month of Sundays have become a miner, and not just because the local coalfields were worked out.

From my bedroom window in High Lane I could see the Chatterley Whitfield colliery. Chatterley Whitfield had closed down, but, in an untypical display of civic enterprise, someone had been fast enough to reopen it as a museum, the first tourist attraction of its type in the country, and Stoke acquired its first brown road sign, pointing the way to the Heritage. In amongst the sprawl of buildings at the pithead, a centre had been set up where the tools of the trade – helmets, lamps, axes, shovels – were displayed in glass cases. Here was the future for the north, a glimpse of the sightseeing industry that would one day come to take the place of work itself. As well as allowing you to contemplate the redundant equipment, the admission ticket bought a further trip underground to examine the rest of the set-up. The lift (the 'cage') plummeted down the shaft at such a rate that it threw your stomach into your mouth: just getting to work was frightening. I had been down there on a day trip, as part of the General Studies element of the course I was completing at the college of further education. My impression of conditions a mile under the surface was that they were cold, dark, claustrophobic and dreadful. Going down once was daunting enough, but imagine this – some men spent their days and lives toiling there, and in clouds of dirt and dust too, not in the unreal quiet in which we crept around in our party of twelve with our tour guide and our visitor passes. The job was unthinkable. For all the braggadocio that chefs display at their stoves, in comparison to mining, cookery is hardly the work of a hard man. Chefs know as much: it's where the braggadocio comes from in the first place. More than a few of my erstwhile school acquaintances let me know about the pansy nature of my career choice on the occasions when I would encounter them on the bus at the end of our respective days. They wouldn't say anything. They would just look at me in a particular way, sitting wrapped in donkey jackets coated with dust from whatever proper graft it was that they'd managed to pick up. Their knapsacks contained empty Thermos flasks and lunchboxes; mine was full of lever arch files and chef's whites. I might even be reading the paperback that I kept for impressing the girls. It was only technical college I was attending, not Oxbridge, but still: it was college; still, I was a college boy, a weed and a wet, with soft skin covering my nice, clean hands.

A few years later, in the battle between the forces of Thatcher and Scargill, when I was arguing the miners' case with the yuppies in my London circle, here was the point I could never get through to them: that the strikers were fighting for the right to get ingrained with dirt, to work in conditions that would be horrible to most people, certainly to the new breed of white-collar coke fiend such as themselves. The point they could never get through to me was that the only good business was a privatised one, and that the only persons who should yield any fiscal power, or were fit to take profit in this society, were risk-taking entrepreneurs like them, not the everyday proles on whose backs they were busy parcelling up share issues for their get-rich-quick schemes. Even though in other circumstances, when we weren't arguing about the industrial civil war that was going on in the north – when we were stretched over a snooker table, or having our eardrums shattered at gigs, or dancing, drinking, smoking and getting stoned – I might actually like some of these individuals, and vice versa, I could never *be* one of them. When it came down to it, we were on opposite sides, though they might sometimes imagine it could be otherwise.

As with Henry, my affair with the yuppies was another dysfunctional relationship. But it wasn't as though I got nothing out of either of these associations. Henry taught me how to make Lobster Thermidor, for instance, a trick that can be used as an effective seduction technique, given the right girl, if the copy of *The Great Gatsby* has failed. There's a long-winded recipe for Lobster Thermidor. Not necessary.

Method for Henry's Lobster Thermidor:

Get chef to prepare a lobster.
Impress stepson, or girl, by cracking claws with your teeth to reveal the sweetest meat.
For drama, mention something about how you've already removed the poisonous part.
Arrange the claw meat over the rest of the soft flesh along the shell, coat with cheese sauce* and grill.

* Method for Henry's Cheese Sauce:
Pour a pint or two of double cream into a pan, grate in half

a pound of Cheddar, add salt and pepper, and a spoonful of English mustard. Warm gently until it becomes thick and sauce-like.

To serve:
Flambé with cognac which you have warmed in a ladle over a fire.

As for what I gained from my deal with the yuppies, well, they were something to loathe, for a start, which is at least energizing. In the mid-nineties I was watching Martin Amis on a TV show. Amis was an author I greatly admired for a while, for *Money* and for *London Fields*. He was bemoaning the fall of Thatcher in terms of her usefulness to literature: she invigorated the writers of this country by providing them with something to revile, he said. At that point I was a nascent writer myself. I found his analysis both encouraging and discouraging at the same time; I had plenty of hatred in me, but Thatcher had gone. The kind of hatred I go in for, though, is a brand that is easily tempered, or suspended, provided that I am kept amused. For instance, the diaries of the Tory reprobate Alan Clark kept me alive through a stag weekend in Amsterdam held on behalf of one of the yuppies (I abhor stag dos, they are so basic, predictable and *long*). Though I was opposed to more or less everything that he stood for, I warmed to Clark more than to most members of the stag party, or to any Labour parliamentarian I could bring to mind. He had charm, and made attempts at self-knowledge, which all counts for something. I liked him for his endearing, Pooterish attempts at exonerating himself from his own loutish behaviour, and for his appetites for art and drinking and womanizing and cars.

My yuppies provided me with some splendid larks on their own account too, though. I am happy to drink if I am not forced to do it for forty-eight-hours solid in the service of preparing some poor sop for marriage. Down by the river near Hammersmith Bridge where the pubs are strung out in a convenient line of half a dozen, each a short walk apart, I participated in many a yuppie pub crawl. Pissed and stoned, pulling each other's undercrackers down and offering out dares and challenges – to hurdle impossible obstacles, leading to broken bones, and falls into the Thames – they offered a diversion of a new type to me. They were rugger-buggers, and I ought to have despised them all the more for that, but somehow I didn't. They enabled me to feel loose and free, and I regarded them as fun and as a proper entertainment. Occasionally I got involved, of course, but for much of the time I was a spectator to these escapades, which often served as default devices to allow them to settle scores from their boarding-school days. Most pertinent, for me, was that they let me into their gang. For that I almost loved them more than I hated them, but beyond either of these two (related) responses, I *needed* them.

As I started to understand London, I began to work out that to become a person who counted *in any way at all* required a substantial upgrade on the first world in which I lived, the bed-sit-land that spreads off Earl's Court Road, an invisible territory occupied by a refugee army of itinerant shift workers. You could live there for ever, in rented accommodation, without anyone knowing you had ever existed. Every so often you'd read a story in a free sheet about a person who had died, and that it was only a bad smell that alerted the outside world to the body weeks after the death. No one had knocked at their door, no one from their workplace had bothered to look in on them to see if they were alright; no one cared. That would never happen in the north.

To safeguard against a fate of this sort I called home every week. I used the public phone boxes at the end of the street. There was always a queue. The interiors were festooned with business cards advertising the fantastic services of Spanky Sue and Mistress Whippy. I used to wonder about calling those numbers, but instinct told me that they probably looked much better in the pictures on the cards than would turn out to be the case, face to face. Also I was much too scared. In Stoke-on-Trent services such as these were just pretend; the ads were taken out without the provider's knowledge or consent: *so and so is a slag, phone this number for sex.*

The walk to the phone box and back allowed me a glimpse into a parallel universe where dinner parties took place in the basement kitchens and ground-floor dining rooms of restored Victorian terraced houses. Here people lived lives that did not take place in a single purple pad measuring ten foot by twelve foot with a sink in the corner. Here people mingled as if they had known each other for years. It was as if this was their real life. It was as if the streets off the Earl's Court Road were real homes. I would pause and glance through the windows, watching the silent clink of wine glasses and the mime of small talk as dishes of olives were passed, and I would wonder how you could ever make it into that clan. Our separate cultures existed in intimate geographical proximity but we were united only by a postcode; in any other measurable sense we were worlds apart. To move from one world to the other required luck, and an act of some sort, a *turn*. I'd discover this much, one day.

But that was the future. I had not met those yuppies yet.

For the moment I was still on the train south, the barren mines and all the rest of the industrial death of my home behind me, the best place for it.

I made my way down to the buffet car where individual pies filled with Bramley apple purée were on sale in individual flat boxes. The choice was between these or British Rail sandwiches, sandwiches with a single sliver of processed cheese pressed between two slices of Mother's Pride scraped down with margarine. British Rail sandwiches were the butt of jokes told by those racist television comedians, alongside their standard repertoire of gags about mothers-in-law, blacks and Irishmen called Paddy.

> Q. What's the fastest game in the world?
> A. Pass the parcel in a Belfast pub.

Everybody used to tell that one. The year of my departure was 1980 but the new decade hadn't opened yet; to all intents and purposes it was still the seventies.

I had graduated with an Ordinary National Diploma (OND) in Hotel, Catering and Institutional Operations. This qualification, in addition to a reference from the principal of the department at college, was enough to get me the job with the Savoy Group, even if I had turned up wearing a Jam T-shirt and an Iranian Army surplus jacket accessorized with a CND badge. After the interview, I made my way from the Strand over to Mayfair– another name from the Monopoly board – to look at Claridge's Hotel, which was where I was to be stationed. I paused by the polished brass door plates of private art dealers, and looked into the windows of extraordinary specialist shops: a milliner's, a game dealer, a gentleman's parfumier. On one corner stood a casino with a gold portico and black mirrored doors; outside it a concierge with braided epaulettes paced up and down; across the road a long stretch of plate glass protected a showroom full of Rolls Royces, outside which was another concierge, this one patrolling the pavement while wearing a top hat. Young men in suits, brogues and ties marched headlong as if they meant business. Every second car was a Jaguar or a Bentley. I suddenly felt tatty, and, I suppose, for the first time in my life, very out of place.

One month after the interview I left Stoke for the second time and for real. The position I had been offered was as a management trainee. The Savoy Group consists of the exclusive quartet of hotels that includes the Connaught and the Berkeley as well as date varied with each telling, as did his age. He was about forty-five, I'd say, a good decade older than Mother, as he called our mother.

'Watch out, Mother's coming,' he would warn.

Or more typically, the maudlin version, accompanied by a Spanish guitar and a dab of the teary eye: 'Mother is a good a mother, and remember you only ever have a one a mother.'

Henry's English was ropey and his accent was so impenetrable that, once I had my ear tuned in, I was often required to interpret for him.

'What's he saying?' friends, relatives and the general public would ask, as if he wasn't there, as if he could no more understand them than vice versa.

'Is he a Paki?' someone from Manchester once asked Mother on a beach in the South of France: Henry's pigmented skin had deepened to a richer tone under the Mediterranean sun. Mother and Henry were pioneers of the early package holiday. We had travelled by 24-hour non-stop coach and were staying in a caravan park opposite the bay of St Tropez. The Mancunian's question gave us all a laugh, principally because it drove Henry mad ('I am from a-Barcelona not from a-fucking Pakistan!') and sent him into one of his regular bouts of juvenile petulance in which he sulked like a girl. The question itself is a disgrace, of course, but I remember disregarding that; it's a query that adequately represents the everyday colloquial British racism which has already been mentioned, with which we are all too familiar, a racism that's beyond reason, that's uncorrectable. Where would you start?

'No, our stepfather is not a Paki.'

'What is he then? A dago wop?'

'That's right. Next?'

Henry was, though, in turn, and in many ways, a disgrace in his own right. He once jumped up and down on Bumble's

Claridge's, and the flagship in the Strand. I could not, on these shores, have fetched up in any environment that was more strikingly at odds with my existence to date, nor more antithetical to my general mindset and political stance; not even a placement as a footman at Buckingham Palace would have thrown me into a society where the social distinctions were so various, so many, so well observed and so complex.

Ostensibly it was guests who topped the status structure. Guests were sub-divided, in ascending order, as follows:

The ordinary indecent rich
The VIP indecent rich
The American indecent rich
European royalty
Hollywood royalty

And then there was an elite category for those with serious money: Arabs.

Beyond Arabs were the super-rich, persons who had more elite money than could ever be counted: Arab royalty.

This pecking order was recognised by the staff on the basis of tipping. Arabs seldom looked at what they were handing over; they would drop fifties as easily as tens or twenties, and could spread notes like confetti. If it was your lucky day, you could pick up more in tips from Arabs than you earned a week in wages (£50, which was distributed in cash in brown envelopes on a Friday). Upon hearing of the arrival of an Arab party, staff perked up like trail hounds set free from their kennels. Waiters would fly to open doors, offering to polish shoes before the valets – snoozing in their quarters – had caught up with events on the ground. The Assistant General Manager would arrive with a sweep, swatting waiters out of his path. He would proceed to put on a master class in obsequiousness and fawning. It was something to see, in its way. As was the aftermath; the sneer of disdain directed towards the disappearing flock of thobe-clad, sandal-wearing, towel-heads. Management's attitude extended to persons even beyond those from the Middle East: in their own eyes they were superior to almost all those whom they served.

But never mind about guests – guests were here today and gone tomorrow. The pecking order on the staff side was where it counted.

The General Manager was never seen. He was a recluse who lived in a penthouse office from where he ruled over his court of senior managers, middle managers, and junior managers: watch your back. The consensus amongst the worker groups was that junior management were the worst of a bad lot, as bent as a four pound note. By this we meant that they were corrupt, but we also meant that they were gay too. Their sexuality, however, generated less than the usual amount in the way of disapprobation: even the minority cult of straights such as myself were metrosexual enough to consider a gay friend (who was not a corrupt junior manager) to be a cool accessory. The thought crosses my mind that those friends I have retained, or the friendships I have restored, or those I have more recently made with people from my home town, work like this: I am a gay(er) friend to them. I am not the same as them anymore, but that does not mean that I am not without interest, the interest being that I represent a range of ideas and ideals that have no connection with either real life as she is lived, or with my beginnings. I am a specimen, an example of something 'a bit weird'. They suspect me of being a supporter and advocate of all sorts, from keeping a secret man-bag to visiting displays of modern art and then, worse, wittering on about it: talking about a pickled shark in the reverent, earnest and gruesome argot of the Islington chin-stroker. They may not have heard me use the term 'post-modern' but they know I am capable of it: the white wine business, which they have seen with their own eyes, more than once, proves as much. And then there is the stuff I eat.

'What the fuck is that supposed to be?' one of them says as he shields his eyes from the sight of a vase of yogurt, nut clusters and fruit sauce that I have purchased in a café.

Whatever it is, it's not a bacon butty. How it can be that I have the gall to be seen in charge of such an item in their presence without even having the decency to look particularly ashamed is beyond the beyonds. My way of being is removed and perverse. The mockery is a one-way street; I do not mock them back. How could I? It is *I* who have changed, not them. I could avoid them, of course. But I do not, because I like them, and I like being with them, even though when they make me a cup of tea, I know it will come ready-sugared, that is with three sugars as standard, take it or leave it.

A group from Stoke organise, and invite me on, a trip to Berlin, a long weekend. I order a bottle of Chablis to wash my dinner down, a bottle I share with another one like me, from Stoke too, another who ought to know better. There are five of us in total: two middle-class disgraces, three working-class heroes.

'Fuck me, they'll be *talking* about it in a minute,' says one hero vis-à-vis the wine.

'Please no,' says Lee, the second of the heroes, brother of the other disgrace.

'Oooh, a heady note of tarmac and custard,' says Old Stokie, our guide and chaperone.

And they all cock their little pinkies amusingly as they lift their manly beers. There is pleasure in it for them, the mockery, a pleasure we middle classes grandly make allowances for, and bravely take on the chin.

We are forced, me and middle-class Elt, brother of Lee, into ordering another bottle. Of Chablis. And then we move on to some sort of fruit-flavoured lager, to show we are hard, that even if we can't stomach beer while we eat our tea, somewhere within us we can still access an earlier self. In fact, more than that, we start ordering schnapps chasers to accompany the raspberry beer – now we are showing off. In the morning while we will experience the abyss in the form of our hangovers, they won't.

There are any number like Elt and I (he runs his own communications business), mid-lifers with mutable roots, one foot in the culture of the here and now, one foot in the culture of the there and then. Anyone who has ever lived in London for more than five minutes will have bumped into the disorientated beginner type. There's one in every pub, issuing advice about how the ale is cheaper and better back home, where the women are more beautiful and more willing, and also, while they're about it, how is it that you can't buy decent black pudding in a so-called capital city which in any case is full of shandy-swilling nonces and other assorted poufs? Of London's population of ten million, ten per cent consists of chippy northerners and other assorted chippy types: they come in from all points: north, south, east and west, from any destination beyond the Home Counties.

Back home, the failed beginner type will have the following to say, to anyone who is interested: 'I lived in London once: absolute, utter fucking shithole.'

He may omit to mention that his experience lasted nine whole days, nine of which were spent camped out on a friend's floor in Tooting Bec, and that this was as much as he could take of the nightly disdain that greeted his skinful banter, roaming hands and his rendition of 'Hey Big Spender' as he swayed along the tube train which took him back and forth between Tooting Bec and Trafalgar Square (where he had discovered this great Bierkeller full of Swedish birds, with an all-night happy hour).

'Spend a little time with me...'

Our hero signs off with a high leg-kick and a pirouette that lands him on his backside. I have seen it with my own eyes. Finding his act greeted by a grim silence and a round of no-applause, he offers the following commentary: 'Snotty cows, the lot of yous. You've lost out here… big time… that's the last you'll see of *me*.' I have heard it with my own ears. And he means it, too. Soon enough he's on his way back, to Glasgow, to Wrexham, to Burnley.

The brave little soldiers who find it in themselves to persist through this awkward period, those who bed in and step up to the plate (who may, in time, even come to use that hackneyed expression) begin, as a matter of survival, to evolve.

'He's changed in *himself*,' his mother will say, if asked, and she will shake her head sadly. What happened to the nice, *normal* boy she once knew?

He has retained a mental image of returning home, is what.

He has pictured the bus journey to the dole office and the grubby little vacancies advertised in the attached job centre offering manual work at rates of pay that make it more profitable to stay in bed, is what. If there are even any of *those* jobs left.

These are the images that have halted him when he has felt homesick. These are the images that have fuelled him. These are the images that have enabled him to stick it out. This is what has happened to him.

And now he has only gone and cemented his relationship with his new self by becoming the type of person who has got a foot on the property ladder, who has purchased a very small flat for many, many thousands of pounds a mile or two from Wandsworth Common, and who, first things first, has taken the doors to be dipped and then hired an industrial sander to strip the floorboards.

'He's changed in *himself*: he hasn't even got any carpets now.'

*****

London Calling

I take my children everywhere, but they always find their way back home.

It's an old gag, one which turns on the permanent present relevance of its universal truth.

Even before it degenerates into nostalgia (a word which expands when the etymology is checked: it's from the Greek *nostos*: return home, and *algos*: pain), there is the compulsion to go back, to see where you stand, to take a measure on the distance between the *ingénu* you so recently were and the cutting-edge avant-garde vegan reformer you have become – an individual who might possibly deny ever meeting the former version of himself, depending on the company he was in.

The obvious method of taking this reading is to enter an old stomping ground.

'Not being funny, but you look a bit of a twat,' an old school friend (the boy whose parents were the first to be divorced) said to me in a pub in Stoke about eighteen months after I'd left. He made his observation three pints into our conversation. He'd put some weight on since I had last seen him, the majority of which consisted of Bass. The prompt for his comment (I had noticed him repeatedly eyeing it) was the 1950s three-quarter-length Italian overcoat I was wearing. It was a brown mohair check with a mottle effect and a slightly hairy finish, like a rug. In my view, it was totally hip, as were all second-hand overcoats, resonant as they were of Echo and the Bunnymen, Joy Division, and all the rest of the overcoat-wearing indie band fraternity (some of their music was not entirely to my taste, but they were northern, ergo they were from my tribe, and their outfits were beyond reproach). I had purchased the garment from a second-hand stall on Camden Market for twenty quid. Camden Market was a bazaar where you could buy an alfalfa burger from a van parked next to a stall spread with boxes of seven-inch singles, next to another selling vintage woodworking tools, next to one selling Georgian fireplace tiles, next to another selling bongs and head gear. Camden Market was nothing like the Victorian market hall in Stoke.

I visited Camden a few months after I started work for the Savoy Group. I alighted at the tube station called Chalk Farm, a name which to my ears had the exotic ring of Joni Mitchell, Lower Manhattan, Bleecker Street. I had read about the place in *Time Out*. None of my fellow workers shopped there; they all seemed to stick to Oxford Street. I walked around the area wearing my new overcoat for the whole of the day following its purchase. The Camden Town – Kentish Town – South Hampstead district was my first real encounter with Bohemia. There had been one alternative-type music venue in Stoke (in the nearby town of Newcastle-under-Lyme, to be accurate) called the Bridge Street Arts Centre. That was a dismal hole frequented by two old men who were too miserly even to own a dog between them.

Camden Market has become a theme park in the intervening years, a sanitised tourist trap repackaged into a Lego-built hall with running water; when I first saw the place it was a stinking shanty town peopled by a United Nations of soap-dodgers, drug addicts, wannabes and a colony of Irish tramps (Arlington House, the dossers' refuge made famous by the Madness song 'One Better Day' is just round the back). Heading south from Chalk Farm towards the market, I might have been entering Tangier for all that the territory resembled any other part of England I had set eyes on before. Whether the eighties had opened or not made no difference to Camden Market: here it was still the sixties. Though punks and mod revivalists were evident in numbers, the dominant cult groups were the hippy and the ex-hippy. The air flickered with the notes of many competing strains of dope smoke. And this in the *daytime*. I was amazed. In context my overcoat had been a staid, conservative purchase: I had been compelled to buy *something* to blend me in, to allow me to seem less of an incongruous, provincial ned.

Back home, the reverse applied. There was no realistic come-back on the first divorced boy's observation of my appearance in my coat. And in a way, I was happy to hear it; it confirmed to me what I already knew, that I was heading in the right direction and making a go of my life. I would use that same pub repeatedly over the early years, on my visits home, dressed in my style of the day. Just a look, a glance, would do me: in this way I could keep a private aesthetic account that I could convert into something else, a complicated register of cultural superiority. The more I could be identified as abnormal for Stoke, without standing out like a sore thumb (by wearing my hair in dreadlocks, for instance, and accessorising with Rasta-wear, a style Bumble adopted when he followed me to the capital a few years later: 'Is he performing in a show?' someone asked Mother when he accompanied her outdoors), the happier I was.

And though, of course, I held the opposing view regarding which one of us looked a bit of a twat in the pub that night, it was my old friend, the first divorced boy, who was correct on the matter; no question. His choice of coat was an anorak from Millets Camping. Everybody's choice of coat was an anorak from Millets Camping. I fished in my pocket for my ciga-rettes, a packet of Camel Filters, which drew another look of disgust. I had become such a posing git that I could not even smoke a proper fag any more.

Later, back at home, I offered Henry a Camel Filter. He looked at me curiously and held out his Bensons. When I declined, he became agitated.

'They not paying you enough to afford a Bensons down there? Come on Stephens, ask for a rise – you no hafta smoke them things, surely?'

Camel Filters were more expensive than Bensons, but there was no mileage in mentioning this fact. He had arrived at his point of view, and that was a that. We sat smoking our separate fags, an emblem of the way things had become. But he always put *Carmen* on the record player and pulled out the monogrammed handkerchief as I packed my stuff to get back on the road to London.

'The door is always open for you here, Stephens, remember that.'

It was a nice thing to say, Camel Filters or no Camel Filters, a generous way of expressing another saying, the flip side of the old gag: *Home is the place that, when you go there, they have to take you in.*

Hopefully, it won't come to that, though, because the horrors to be found on return visits are many and varied and become more profound as the years pass. On a trip to a friend's parents in Wigan when we were in our late thirties, I was fed dinner (that is, lunch) at a table set neatly with a cloth and place mats. The main course was meat pie, chips and tinned peas; a pot of tea and rounds of Mother's Pride and margarine to accompany, followed by tinned fruit and Wall's ice cream. Drinking, as in drinking, was allowed only after the meal was finished. The booze came in the form of cans of Ace, which is a cheap supermarket lager, not wholly unpotable, but not the best available either, not by some distance.

It was an ordeal. The food worried me; it was too heavy for the time of day, and completely the wrong stuff; it would certainly cause disruption to the finely tuned eco-world that is my digestive tract: one symptom of becoming a middle-class type is that the years spent eliminating certain items from, and generally refining, your diet, mean that you end up with a system that will not function correctly unless it receives regular small dishes of roquette, or similar foreign salad leaves dressed with extra-virgin olive oil, frequent lubrications of San Pellegrino, portions of pasta garnished with fresh shavings of Parmigiano Reggiano,

and a plentiful supply of chilled bottles of white. You would order a cup of tea with your lunch as soon as you would a Lemsip.
And you may ask yourself, well, how did I get here?
How the hell did you become the sort of person who cannot eat an ordinary Fray Bentos steak-and-kidney pie out of a tin without worrying about the detrimental side effects it might have on subsequent bowel movements and general body humours?

You did it by going through a sequence of manoeuvres which saw you, at one point discard ordinary food entirely in favour of brown rice, hummus, dates, carrot cake and all the rest of that chick-pea based roughage. But that's not so bad, in itself; who amongst us hasn't had a scrape with vegetarianism? During one period of the mid-'eighties, when radical feminism was at its height but when I had passed through my non-meat-eating phase, I used sometimes to *pretend* to be a vegetarian if I took the view that it might help me get into the knickers of a feminist girl. It was one of my missions in life to find out what feminists were really like when it came down to traditional conditions of engagement (they could not all be lesbians, the law of averages said as much). What would they make of you, the enemy, under such loaded circumstances as those involving rolling around under a duvet in a squat in Muswell Hill? The answer – you could spare yourself a lot of work here, were you not so fevered at the prospect of conquest, were you not so curious – was obvious: they demanded multiple orgasms, and belittled you if you were not capable of providing a plentiful supply of them. Even when you performed until your tongue bled (or was this menstrual blood? – that is, after all, their favourite time of the month to take you down there) and your finger cramped, they would still be happy to let you know, over the post-coital roll-up, that their girlfriend was better at it, more accomplished and sensitive, just more, you know, *empathetic.*

'Perhaps that's because your girlfriend is a lesbian and has had much more practice at the oral and digital than me with my straightness and my instinct for the missionary position,' I said, to the feminist I had latched up with at a miners' benefit gig. Her name was Lottie.

'No darling, she's *bi*.' Lottie replied. There was no answer to that. Bi was just too outré to even consider competing against.

The rest of our post-coital chat would involve Lottie conducting a seminar about how the whole system of patriarchy and female subjugation was my fault. I discovered, as I listened (and I paid attention), that, as a matter of fact, when it came down to it, I was to blame for everything from famine, apartheid, and nuclear proliferation, to the very many juggernauts that belched out toxic diesel fumes all along the Holloway Road. After the lecture and the little spliff, more multiple orgasms were demanded. One might get a bit bored of this and start looking around the place. There was not much to see, just a single poster blu-tacked to the woodchip advising: No Truck with the Chilean Junta! After all this you might be rewarded with a glass of organic elderflower juice and a request to put a shelf up. You are a *man* after all; you must be some use with a tool.

It's not the experimenting with eating alfalfa and bean sprouts *per se*; it's what it leads to.

Gradually you find yourself abandoning mainstream movies in favour of French *noir,* experimenting with pretending to like art-house bands (which can lead to *actually* liking them), alternating your clothing between a Mao and a Che t-shirt, seeking out benefit gigs for Solidarność, and scouring listings magazines in order that you might be advised of where everything *alternative* is happening: alternative clubs, theatre, music, comedy, restaurants, river cruises, bars, the lot. This signposts a route that will find you in a pub in Crouch End one Sunday lunchtime with a glass of Moosehead in one hand, a one-skinner in the other, and a Norwegian jazz quintet on stage; a Norwegian jazz quintet is about as far removed from a Fray Bentos steak-and-kidney pie as it's possible to get without wigging out to Philip Glass. You have reached a crisis point.

Who the hell are you now?

How *did* you get here?

First things first; you needed an intro into that other London, that world of dinner parties that existed in the same streets as your purple room. You needed to meet someone who was not a hotel guest or an assistant manager, nor a regular hotel worker drone either.

There are two kinds of hotel worker drone, one: itinerants like you, holed up in bedsits and staff hostels; two: the locals who actually come from London. The latter might look like a way in, but they are not. They don't want you there in the first place, do they, because, as a matter of fact, they resent you for being the type of person "oo 'as come an' nicked jobs off o' their fambily and kin.' They are not shy of telling you about it either, whilst putting in a very poor impersonation of your accent (no, you do not sound like Paul McCartney).

Say 'book' they ask, so they can laugh at the way you sound the oo. Say 'bath' they ask, so they can laugh at the way you rhyme it with cat, rather than calf.

'Where is Stoke-on-Trent, anyway?' they ask. 'Is it near Newcastle?'

'Well actually, it's near somewhere called Newcastle-under-Lyme...' you begin, only to be interrupted –

'What, there's more than one Newcastle? I fort it was all the same up norf.'

Give up, spare yourself the pointless exercise. It's easier that way.

But, as it's not all the same up norf, neither is it all the same darn sarf either. Although these Cockneys appear to be local, they are not; not really: the London they inhabit lies a dozen or more miles away and is called Wood Green, or Forest Gate, or Catford. They live there with their mum, in something called a maisonette. There was a moment when you imagined that the class bond would unite you with your southern brother, but you would be some way out with that one. Your southern brother, you discover, harbours rather different ambitions to you. He has been travelling into central London every day of his working life and, not unnaturally, he wants a piece of it; he wants dough, birds, glamour, fancy motors and more dough. Aside from his rabid support of the Arsenal or the Spurs, material possessions represent the zenith of his aspirations. Culture is of no consequence to him whatsoever, with the exception of the musical *Cats* which 'makes a fortune, innit; it's a facking cash machine, that'.

It may take you a week or two to work out what it is you have landed yourself in, because in your view such a group should never exist. They are working class, but they are of a breed you have not encountered before, operating a different value system to any one you have previously known. There is something wrong, sinister and evil about them – they are exactly the sort of southerners you can, as it turns out, find it only too easy to despise. They are more than capable of getting your northern knee jerking away like clockwork in very short order, if you let them get to you. What you have here, you suddenly realise, is a base horde that you thought was a myth created by the *Sun*, a newspaper you boycott. What you have here are ordinary persons who have marked their cross next to the Con candidate. They are not even that unaffiliated brand of waster, the floating voter; they are much, much worse than that: they are *working-class Tories*. It is they who have delivered Margaret Thatcher to her throne.

But there is a better retort available than a knee-jerk, if you can only access it – your sense of moral superiority can be channelled into a more useful and adaptable commodity than that crude response: it can be converted into inverted snobbery.

In the service of self-preservation, in the protection and preservation of your confidence and psyche, inverted snobbery is your suit of armour on this journey. Or at least, it's your overcoat, as you have already discovered, in the pub back home: reinverted inverted snobbery is the name of the game you were testing out there, imagining you could turn up wearing an item like something from the *Italian Job*, the consequence of which was a foregone conclusion. You showed promise though, trying it on in such a manner. It was snobbery reinverted and put into action, a demonstration to yourself that, properly cultivated, this attitude will allow you to slide anything, and anybody, beneath your dignity.

Q. What is he after, your southern wide-boy colleague? When it comes down to basics, what does he *really* desire? A. A Lamborghini, a Page 3 stunna, a box at Highbury, and a mansion in Epping.

Whereas the furthest he's going to get, with a bit of ducking and diving, is an Escort XR3i, a hairdresser's assistant called Shaz, a season ticket for the North Bank, and he'll actually move further *away* from his des res until he finds a housing estate in the London Borough of Redbridge, where he can afford the price of a three-bed-semi Tudor-style home built by Freddy Barratt. Here, deep in the retrograde county of Essex, he will be able to share his racist views with his neighbour Norman Tebbit, and vote Tory or BNP to his heart's content. He will be 'well into' a terrible music cult called jazz funk which will require him to wear pink Pringle sweaters and have his hair cut into 'a wedge'. Now that you have seen his future in this way, you are in a position to test out your killer line.

'I'm *not interested in money*.'

The eighties comedy stereotype, the plasterer 'Loadsamoney', was derived from thousands of prototypes, and here you have one standing before you now, your Cockney/Essex-wide-boy bellhop, laughing until his sides ache at your appalling faux pas. He will call you a few choice names for it. He will remind you of the matter at every available opportunity: 'There he goes, the monkey: not interested in money.'

For evermore he will go out of his way to pass by your pantry, wafting his wad in your face in the aftermath of a good tipping. But how can that impress you, given your stated position, in respect of 'the folding?'

It cannot.

By discarding Mammon, you have moved yourself out of one specific line of fire. At the same time you have also given yourself the distinction of seeking higher pleasures than those available on grub street; you have acquired (in your own mind, at any rate) intellectual elevation. What you are interested in is *ideas,* a point you can quite easily prove by returning to that interminable Bernard Levin sentence in *The Times,* or better still, by flaunting the *NME.*

'What the fack is that sposed to be?' your friend will ask, grimacing at a cover shot of Vini Reilly, Ian Curtis or some other grey northern drone who does not wear a pink V-neck sweater and a fat identity bracelet and is not absolutely kicking for Frankie Beverley and Maze.

Actually, I grew to love this jazz funk music, once I had calmed down – both for itself and because, like conjuring up a Lobster Thermidor, dropping a twelve-inch 'platter' of funk could turn out to be a seductive move, even with some feminists, and was certainly worth a try with more regular soul sisters. In any case we had always had black music in Stoke, most particularly in the clubs the Heavy Steam Machine and the Torch, dance halls that were key spots on the Northern Soul circuit, a scene that was before my time, though I had heard of it, in legend. But everyone's older sister played Tamla Motown while dolling-up to go out on a Friday night. And that was not all. Before I left Stoke for good I had seen both The Three Degrees and The Supremes at the cabaret club, Jollees, which was situated on top of the bus station in Longton (one of the six towns). Jollees existed in a parallel universe. Set out like Caesar's Palace in tiered arcs of tables with frilled purple lampshades, Jollees specialised in serving up chicken-in-a-basket and exceptionally unlikely performers. The club was the brainchild of a local impresario who, through a gift of genius, persuaded Matt Monro, Tom Jones and other cabaret greats that Stoke-on-Trent was the Vegas of the Midlands. When the nightclub eventually fell out of fashion, it reinvented itself, becoming widely known as the venue that hosted the annual World Darts Championships, during those years when Jocky 'On the Oche, at Jollees' Wilson was at his peak. It made me melancholy to see this, on national television. It made me think things were going downhill, that my home city was making a show of itself. Darts is the most reductive of popular entertainments. Darts is played and watched by an army of shell-suited fat bastards. Darts is not Diana Ross singing, *Touch me in the morning, then just walk away, we don't have tomorrow, but we had yesterday.*

My response to seeing Jocky on the Oche consisted of a feeling of faint nausea tinged with a deep, sad embarrassment.

This wasn't just inverted snobbery; this was actual snobbery. I was on my way.

*****

So. Back in central London experience quickly teaches you that you will find no common bond with either strand of your fellow worker, neither the itinerant nor the local. And climbing into bed with management would only get you so far: the Assistant

General Manager at the Berkeley kept a small rented flat in Barons Court, a fact that circulated in our domain. It was important to know how high you might rise, if you fancied the look of the ladder, and *that* was not far enough, not for all the years of servility you'd have to put yourself through to get there.

So. The logical thought insinuates itself: to escape bedsit-land you need to make the acquaintance of the strand of native who inhabits the real London, the London you see around you, the London that has nothing to do with hotels but rather the London that is home. You need to meet a householder, a person who has at least that much stake in the city. It is not one of those dinner party guests from the basement flats of Cornwall Gardens, Earl's Court that you are looking for either: they are wrong in every way – they are fogeys, both young and old, rigged up in camel-coloured corduroys with turn-ups, shiny brogues and shirts with cutaway Windsor collars from T.M. Lewin of Jermyn Street. They are alien to you, and they will always remain so; while you have not formed a clear idea of exactly who it is you're looking for, you've formed a certain idea of who it isn't.

In your mind's eye the clan you are seeking to join are something like the bohemians of Camden; not them exactly, but a similar, less cliquey tribe of hipsters. You know they exist. You have purchased a bicycle to save money on tube fares and you have ridden around the city on days off; you have peeked into the postcodes that lie not far beyond the central pocket of extreme wealth. Here, a few miles from Charing Cross, you find street after street of Victorian terraced houses characterised by smartly painted front doors with stained-glass window panels and polished brass knockers. The kind of local you are looking for lives in Fulham, Clapham and Battersea to the south, in Islington, Gospel Oak and West Hampstead to the north.

By not returning home with your tail between your legs after ten days in the capital, by instead taking a look around, you have put yourself on the map, but only just. The most pressing and essential thing now is to get bedded in. To do that you need an introduction to this other world.

Part Two: Something to be

An apprentice arrived at work. He was a confident, good-looking boy, in a blond and foppish sort of way. He worked in my department. I had settled in room service because the pay was much better there than the flat £50 basic of the kitchens, where I had started my managerial apprenticeship, and the conditions were considerably less brutal. Hotel kitchens are hot and unpleasant, both physically and psychologically. They are built on huge insecurities which are played out through machismo and aggression. There is constant jockeying for pole position, and fist fighting forms a part of this. Back then the kitchens were hidden down in the basements; they were not the theatres they have become today. Violence was allowed because nobody could see it. It was not for me. Upstairs, battles were more subtle, in that they were verbal. I preferred that.

At first, like everybody else, the blond mocked my accent. But he didn't get much change for his trouble. He didn't get much change because I didn't like him, and I soon worked out why. He was another brand of contemporary I had never encountered until recently: a public schoolboy. He had not got the job by attaining a Diploma or a City and Guilds over two years of study at technical college, nor by turning up on spec and convincing the personnel manager that this was the work he was destined for. He had got the job because his mother knew the Assistant General Manager. This was a brand of overt nepotism taking place in front of my eyes, and the boy didn't even keep quiet about it. He was happy for people to know of his route in, because he thought it cast him in a good light, being well connected in this way. What a complete tosspot.

'It's not what you know, it's who you know.'

I had heard this said a few times in Stoke, but as far as I knew its use was in the abstract; the person mouthing the cliché would be opining as to how life was conducted in government, amongst captains of industry, down south. The person would be talking about matters of which he had no personal experience; the person would be talking rubbish. Well, okay, he might know that *you* had got a job in a restaurant because your stepfather was the maitre d'. But what did that actually mean? It meant you got to bust a gut working split shifts for pin money. It did not mean that you got to work in England's most exclusive hotel group just like that, without obtaining all the qualifications any normal person with ambitions in the field would require, did it? I could just imagine the foppish blond's job interview: 'Oh, I see from this letter of recommendation that you're Gussie Fink-Nottle's boy.'

'Yes, sir.'

'Excellent. When would you like to start?'

*****

Management were all privately educated, as it turned out. As a management trainee I was, theoretically, in line to become a manager of some sort myself. I could never see it happening. Most of them oozed the effortless sense of confidence that I had seldom seen in Stoke, because when asked that most telling of questions, 'Where did you go to school?', they would be able to give the correct and relevant answer by naming a public establishment, albeit a minor one that nobody had ever heard of, Giggleswick or some such. An over-representative sample of public schoolboys appear in this next sequence; I don't know if I gravitate towards them, or they me, or if it is simply that the recently graduated example of the type has a habit of mentioning the matter early on in a potential 'friendship' by saying something about 'school' and then naming the place. I think it's the latter: they identify this game as one in which you cannot participate; they get their one-upmanship in early. That they graduated from the privileged surroundings with a single A level in Geography, attained after three resits, is something they tend to keep quiet about.

The air of hauteur that went with management, then, was not derived from having a brain, but from social association. The sense of self-importance that circulated amongst them was not the simple crass pomposity that may routinely be noted as the accessory of any trumped-up jerk given a title; it was based in genealogy, and it was the first time I had encountered this code. To the best of my knowledge I had never met anyone in Stoke who was inbred in this way. It ought to have incensed me to see the unfairness at play here, to know that these jobs would not be available to my people, not because of their lack of talent, but because of their lack of background. And it did incense me, but not as much as it should have because of a *schadenfreude* that considerably sweetened the pill. These men (they were all men) were required to perform a curiously compromised act in the line of their daily work. Confronted with a guest, management were no more elevated than anyone else, and were required to demonstrate precisely the same level of deference as a Cockney bellboy. And of course, Cockney bellboys and all the rest knew as much, so managers, though they had the usual power of hire and fire, were often to be observed denuded. Like a teacher with a fatal weakness, they lacked any genuine sense of authority, even if they were allowed to rap the bellboy on the head with the back of a silver spoon once the guests were out of sight.

Each worker group had its own internal power structure: the chief doorman had his lieutenant, the lieutenant doorman had his corporal, the corporal doorman had his bellboy. It may look a menial activity, hailing taxis and picking up luggage, but I discovered that the work was (and remains) highly prized, the jobs jealousy guarded. The duties of a doorman have little to do with opening actual doors and everything to do with opening virtual ones. The real job description is that of an agent. A good doorman can procure you a table at the Ivy – tonight – and tickets for any sold-out show in town – also tonight. Guests know this, and the tips are thumping. The world of the door mirrors the masonry of management: no ordinary person can break into it at a grand hotel; the work is distributed on the nod and often runs in families. The junior bellboy is typically the black sheep of the clan. Built like a jockey, he is fantastically elusive: this is because he spends a heavy portion of his time tossing-off members of senior management in return for a smoked salmon sandwich, a Carlsberg 68 and a twenty-pound note.

Other departments may be more democratic, in terms of recruitment, but they all run equivalent internal ranking systems, and beyond the demarcations of rank, each category takes its place in the global pecking order: chefs are superior to waiters; room service waiters consider themselves to have the whip hand over dining room waiters (and vice versa); valets are above chambermaids, often literally. While these two groups simmer with mutual resentment – each blaming the other for uncompleted tasks and treading on each other's toes in the battle for departure tips – it would appear that ironing, laundry and loathing constitute a great aphrodisiac. It was not unusual to find bellboys and other lower orders, like maintenance men, mobbed up with their ears pressed to the linen cupboard door mid-morning, listening in on a knee-trembler and waiting outside at the end to give a round of applause and marks out of ten for artistic interpretation and technical merit.

The reason, by the way, that waiters are superior to maintenance men is that waiters have something of value to trade. A maintenance man may have access to a cupboard full of light bulbs and assorted grommets, but the romantic limitations of such items are plain to see. On the other hand, the fridge in the waiter's pantry is full of wine, beer, champagne, fancy pastries and cakes; he makes sure of this, and such commodities come in useful in the courting of chambermaids and florists, once the valets are out of sight.

It's those who have nothing to bargain with who find themselves at the bottom of the pile: cleaners, potato peelers and *les plongeurs*. Literally translated, *plongeurs* means divers. In Henry's Spanglish kitchen-French, *plongeurs* were dishwashers.

During my time in the job, the BBC news magazine *Nationwide* sent a reporter undercover to pose as a homeless person on the streets of London. In an episode inspired by Orwell's *Down and Out in Paris and London* (this and *Wigan Pier* had become key texts in my library) the journalist was dropped outside Victoria coach station with no money, no change of clothes, nothing; his brief was to exist for a week on that. He was coached in the methods of survival by the tramps and itinerants with whom he spent his first few hours. A group of them led him to the back of one of the big hotels at half past six on his second or third morning, where they queued up in the hope of picking up a day's dishwashing. I was aware of this activity, because I saw it every time I was on an early shift, but the nation was shocked to see filthy vagrants with head lice 'washing up' in the kitchens of landmark five-star hotels, where front-of-house it was top dollar, but behind the scenes it appeared to be all fur coat and no knickers. The programme caused a scandal and signalled the immediate abolition of the practice. Of course, hotels still needed dishwashers, so management turned to the cheapest alternative it could find: sourcing labour from the Bangladeshi community around Brick Lane; the Alis, as they were known, because they all had the same name. Sometimes an Ali would fail to show up and so one floor pantry would call on another to 'borrow an Ali'.

I should have been out of room service by then, continuing my progress as a management trainee, but I settled in because the tips were so good: the choice was between moving on to reception for the flat £50 a week or taking a promotion to *demi-chef de rang* on the floors where I could enjoy a life of relative autonomy and something like £200 a week, £150 of which the taxman never saw. That was good money in 1981; I saved enough to buy a car in just one month. Our Ali was the youngest Ali, with film star good looks, and he spoke the best English of them all too. In idle moments we would talk and smoke. I'd offer him a beer, which, unusually, he accepted; for most, chewing ginseng was their drug of choice. It didn't take Ali long to work out that his people were being paid a third of what we European non-Alis were pulling, and they got nothing out of the tips either, unless we were feeling generous and passed a fiver on. The whole set up was too iniquitous; our Ali turned militant, demanding basic-wage parity, and so, of course, he found himself out on his arse in short order. No one supported him. I was the only one to call for a strike on behalf of the nation of Bangladesh, a suggestion that caused more mirth and derision than my accent, my denunciation of Mammon and my habit of pouring gravy on my chips and eating bread with anything, even pasta, all put together. In catering, it's every man for himself. That was one of the reasons I left the business. That, plus the hours, plus a sense that there must be more to life than this – serving food to people who aren't even hungry in the first place, a fact demonstrated by the amount that came back uneaten and the subsequent sight of bins full of waste when thousands of people were starving in the world. The vulgar excesses of wealth began to make me feel sick. One night a slightly drunken female client sent me out for batteries for her vibrator; she wanted a fuck, clearly, but she wasn't getting it off me. I might be in service, but I wasn't a goddamn prostitute.

I wanted my nights free to chase young girls, not to organize sex aids for corpulent Yankees. And I was keen to pursue all the new kinds of fun that I was discovering with my new friend, the foppish blond privileged boy who, as it turned out, lived in a Victorian terraced house with stained-glass window panels and a polished brass door knocker, off the Fulham Palace Road, SW6.

The Blond lived with his mother. His parents were divorced, which was one thing we had in common. His father, who he seldom saw, lived in the Shires with a woman who looked like a horse, and his mother was often out of the way too, having fun with a distinguished silver-haired man with whom she was having a long-term affair. His mother spoke like the Queen's lady-in-waiting, the distinguished man spoke like David Niven. They were seen out in public together at sporting events like Royal Ascot or the Stella Artois tennis tournament at Queen's; the distinguished man was a BBC correspondent, a founding father of outside broadcast. He was of a rather different order from the majority of our hotel guests: he was an English Gent. I liked him, a lot; he was preternaturally civil and always took a keen interest in our goings on, of which we would keep him informed over the dinners he sometimes treated us to at San Lorenzo's, the old-style Italian restaurant in South Ken (as you learn to call it, now you are a local). I was used to being on the other side of the table, of course. I found it odd, wrong, to be waited on in a place like this. San Lorenzo's was no burger joint; it had a reputation and attracted a certain ilk of celebrity: the Patrick Lichfield and Petula Clark types. Proximity to fame did not faze me, though; we had seen it all in the hotel; it was the best part of the work. On one occasion I took Clint Eastwood his breakfast in bed (scrambled eggs on rye, freshly squeezed OJ, black coffee, all of which struck me as perfect). Every waiter in the place was after that job. I won the prize on the toss of a coin.

I reciprocated the broadcaster's interest in us; I was fascinated by him, and by his situation. I was intrigued by the set-up that he and the Blond's mum had put together: if anyone had an affair in Stoke, then some bloke would get his block knocked off, for sure. There was no way you'd get this quasi-condoned seen-together-in-public idea out of the traps – it would be a complete non-starter. The scene struck me as sophisticated and civilized while at the same time incredible, like being asked to believe in the plot of an Audrey Hepburn movie. Of course, I never asked him anything about any of it as that would have been rude and presumptuous, and he, in turn, proffered no information on his own account. I just observed, that was all. I sang for my supper by being young and by playing the role of northern firebrand, albeit of the kind that could provide amusement without giving offence: I had not learned nothing about manners, deportment and what was U and non-U in the time I had thus far been with the Savoy Group.

His mother's arrangements often left the Blond with the run of the house. The property was furnished in a manner I had never encountered before: traditional and somewhat overblown Victoriana. The fireplaces had pewter metal inserts inset with ornate green tiles, these in turn framed by gothic marble surrounds. On top of the marble a line of RSVP cards was displayed, invitations to 'At homes'. There was a pile of logs in the hearth for burning. Gilded over-mantel mirrors hung on the chimney breast. The sofa (*not* settee – I picked this up quickly, as I had also learned that a serviette is a *napkin*) was fat and beautifully upholstered and spread with many fat and beautifully upholstered cushions. The curtains were full-length, heavy and not only lined, but interlined. When drawn, by cords at the sides, they cushioned the noise of the passing traffic almost completely. Occasional tables in dark wood hosted silver-framed photographs of the Blond and his sister at various ages. The radiators were disguised behind narrow cabinets fronted by lattice-work grilles. The floorboards were not stripped; there was instead a plain carpet over which rugs were laid. The walls were papered in a subtle, delicate pattern based on motifs from the Arts and Crafts movement (I had learned about that in art at school). Nineteenth-century prints hung in the main rooms; on the walls of the toilet there were framed cartoons. I liked the style: it impressed me, it appeared to have intellectual weight; it was thoughtful and it seemed to mean something. Furniture and decoration in Stoke-on-Trent tended to consist of improbable items like a cigarette lighter in the form of a blunderbuss, or a horseshoe threaded with two crossed daggers mounted on a leather plaque, or a nest of three lacquered coffee tables with brass wheels at the reversing end. The only logs came in the form of moulded plastic covers with orange light bulbs underneath to simulate the glow of a fire; the heating was electric. A hammered-copper hood was fixed to the chimney breast, a faux flue to take away the virtual smoke from the electric elements. Nobody went to all the inconvenience of *lighting a fire*. That was the first thing you stopped doing if you were looking to get on in the world.

There was one glaring omission from the Blond's lounge, the centrepiece of any front room in Stoke: the television. But there was one. It emerged for the important matter of watching football, swung out on a bracket from where it was otherwise concealed within a tall corner cabinet. It was too small for watching football in my view, but it was better than nothing; owning a television seemed to be some sort of concession to vulgar society in this house.

Beyond the large lounge – two rooms knocked through –

there was a spacious kitchen with a long, dark dining table with three silver candlesticks. We would sometimes throw dinner parties here, parties in which the Blond's slightly older sister, and others, would join us. The sister was a rock chick. Her boyfriend had been a singer in a seventies rock band and had now gone solo. The conduit by which the Blond and I had got together was music: he had been using the pantry phone to make a personal call to this sister; I overheard him persuading her to sort him out a ticket to see The Clash at the Lyceum in the Strand. This took me aback. I had him down as a Duran Duran fan. I shot him a glance.

'Do you want me to get you one?' he asked, in reply to my glance.

'Yes,' I said.

This was the first culturally switched-on exchange I had experienced since I'd been in London. Forget management; they knew nothing about music. As for the rest of the staff, well, many were Spanish and Italian and so, to all intents and purposes, they were a bunch of Henrys: well clued-up on opera, and that was as far as it went. One of them, Tony, would sometimes bring in a guitar and play flamenco well, and Beatles tunes badly. After the Latinos there were the gays: all big into Abba and Odyssey. Then there was a large Irish contingent from a catering school in Limerick which had a long-standing tradition of supplying staff to the Savoy. Many of these were also gay: more Abba, plus additional Molly Malone and occasional rebel songs when the drinking got going properly. All that was left after that were the jazz-funk-loving bellhops and the Alis. The Alis sometimes sang Hindu prayers to themselves while drying plates and chewing on their ginseng. With the exception of my bad self, there was not a single punk/mod revivalist in the place. The Blond's extraordinary ticket offer was, in a single stroke, enough to override my dislike of him and all that he appeared to stand for.

Something to Be

The Clash were seminal, as the *NME* would say, at the peak of their form: they were the Guns of Brixton and their show was a magnificent challenge to the status quo. They were dressed for battle in khaki fatigues and performed a repertoire of songs that seemed to me to consist of a denunciation of dictator Thatcher in particular, and of right-wing politics in general. Later the band would go out of their way to hinder record company profiteering by ensuring that copies of their triple-disc album *Sandinista!* went out with Pay-No-More-Than £9.99 stickers on it. They were not only putting their fans above the music business, they were being seen to do it. *Sandinista!* contained songs written in support of the rebels in Nicaragua, and of left-wing causes across the globe.

The Blond and I drank a lot on our way to the gig, and the same on the way back; he liked the music, but could do without the politics, he said. Even given this hopelessly misguided and wrongheaded critique, we still managed to do some bonding. It was not until some time later, once I had been fully integrated into his world, that we smoked a joint together. This took place at a dinner party around that long dining table in the kitchen extension. I had never seen drugs before; sniffing the air in Camden Town was as much as I knew about it. When the grass came out after the main course (which I had cooked: a lobster bake, a variation on a Thermidor – singing for my supper, cooking and saying 'book' and 'bath' were my party tricks, my passport), I could not believe my eyes. I was actually frightened. But hold on: these were middle-class kids, living cosy lives in expensive tree-lined streets where the houses boasted stucco window columns and burglar alarm boxes. It *must* be safe. Still, I was reluctant to participate and instead smoked a couple of harmless Camel Filters while the spliff was passed. I sniffed the air again. It was a smell I liked. I watched. The wine had been flowing, as indeed it continued to flow – such changes as might be taking place in my fellow diners as a consequence of their deep inhalations were not so easy to isolate. So I had a few puffs, which had no effect. What a waste of time. So I had a few more puffs to see if anything might actually, y'know, *happen*. Useless. It did nothing.

The next thing I knew it was the following morning. Those who had slept over were awake, brewing coffee and laughing at me.

'It doesn't *do* anything, does it, Foster?'

'How did I get to bed?' I said.

'We carried you up: you had a full whitey.'

'What's a full whitey?' I asked, wondering if this meant that I was dead.

'It's when your eyes roll up so you can only see the whites,' said the Blond, clipping me round the back of the head for being thick enough not to know that.

As far as dope-smoking went they were experts; experts and connoisseurs. The rock chick's friends were a coalition of wasters that she had gathered together from the international departure lounges of the world. They were Australians, Kiwis and white South Africans; they were the global community of surf bums. I don't know whether the Blond's family would have thought of themselves as middle class or upper middle class, which is, in any event, a moot point which cannot be settled without resorting to arcane dissection of family trees, and further assessments based on numerous social indicators. There are, of course, many middle classes – these Fulham dwellers would have little in common with the senior accountant who goes home to a plateful of spag bol in a detached thirties chalet in Solihull and belongs to the local golf club. But, discrete social stratification aside, they were kids who were well ahead of the zeitgeist in certain ways. The rock chick had put her coalition together while on her way to the beaches of California and the streets of San Francisco. She had taken a year out to travel the world a decade before the concept had become the convention that is The Gap Year. The gap year comes second only to the Volvo Estate in standing as a totem for the mainstream middle classes. Roaming the planet in company with an ecologically sound posse of gangstas on a Visa card is probably the most conservative gesture any teenager can make now. It would be less grim (for the rest of society) if there was any escape, but the fact is, there's nowhere to hide. Do something entirely ordinary: fly down for a short break in Crete, and what do you find? You find there's one sat either side of you at the pavement café, busily unpacking and repacking surfwear into a rucksack while blarting away about this great guy they have to contact back in Phuket or whatever, but they've *lost his email* or whatever, and the battery has run out on the phone and now that's been stolen too and so they have to report it to the Policia, which is *so boring,* but they have to, otherwise they won't be able to make a *claim* or whatever. Back in Blighty, here they come again, commandeering seven tables in the beer garden, rolling up matchstick cigarettes, shunning footwear or whatever, while getting on with the key part of the trip: sharing the experience with their immediate circle of a hundred friends. They are not shy of broadcasting their status as mass conformists, that's for sure, but then they do own the world, don't they, and now they've seen it too, why shouldn't they give a running commentary or whatever.

But back in 1981 this notion of the 'right to travel' was something of a new idea, or at least a revival of an old one: the Victorian Grand Tour, an activity that critics had derided for its lack of adventure a century earlier.

'The tour of Europe is a paltry thing, a tame, uniform, unvaried prospect,' said one observer.

Anyone who has seen *A Room with a View* will get the point, and it seems that little has changed in this particular rite of passage, with the exception of the destinations involved: I make it my business never to ask any young person about their experiences in Thailand.

But in the rock chick's case her pioneering adventures had the splendid side effect of introducing her into the supply line of some of the most exclusive marijuana known to man. Ausies, Kiwis and white South Africans, I discovered, specialised in the field of dope-smoking. Add in the surf bum element – more specialists – then super-enhance with a seventies rock band boyfriend – a career dope-smoker – and what do you end up with? You end up with some dude parcelling up weed in Haight-Ashbury and posting it via airmail to be picked up from a PO Box in Willesden Green, man, that's what. You end up – or in my case you begin – with the dope equivalent of a 1958 Dom Perignon laced with bootleg Russian vodka, the stuff that makes you go blind.

Once I'd discovered ganja, I smoked it a lot. For a time, no event was complete without a spliff – a wedding, a funeral, a job interview, a flight, a run in the park – all of this, it seemed to me, could be enhanced by dope. The car I bought with my room service money was a black Mini with a white vinyl roof, bull bars, and tinted-out windows. I purchased it from a fellow employee at the hotel, a soul boy. It was a car that had been pimped before car-pimping had been heard of, and it was a vehicle that enabled me to learn at first hand what a bunch of racists the Metropolitan Police are. I used to get pulled in it at least three times a week. Through the tinted-out windows they could only guess, but it was bound to be driven by a black man. Once they discovered me inside, they lost all interest, made up some excuse about a dodgy brake light and waved me on. Had they bothered with even the most cursory of investigations, they would often have been in a position to add to the crime figures: being the only one of us with wheels, and being thrilled to drive around London in my new car, I was always ferrying dope around for friends.

I would sometimes manage a weekend off and drive back to Stoke on a Friday night, a journey I'd always begin with a joint. I was a dimwit and complacent and I am lucky to be alive: while it wasn't quite *Fear and Loathing in Las Vegas,* I'd often overshoot the junction where the M1 meets the M6 because I was busy tripping out to my latest C60 compilation, or because I was racing a fat man in a Ford Granada, or because I was zoning off on a cosmic tangent or randomly giggling at the memory of a scene from *National Lampoon's Animal House.* In this way I'd end up driving home via a village in Leicestershire called Ashby-de-la-Zouch, a place name that would assume hilarious proportions, causing a further wrong turning and transforming a three-hour journey into one that took more than five. But, hey, wasn't that all part of the fun, and hey, wasn't I even *cooler* than fuck now that I had a couple of packets of Rizlas and a stash in the inside pocket of the Italian overcoat?

I'd make my way to the Elephant and Castle pub in Fegg Hayes, a council estate, a good council estate, more or less. The landlady of the Elephant sometimes used to bring her pet down on a Saturday night as a kind of on-the-house entertainment. Her pet was a python – it laced around her shoulders and bosoms as she pulled pints. This was a spectacle that did not mix well with dope: this was a spectacle that succeeded brilliantly at freaking me out.

But in general terms I was safe in the Elephant because my girlfriend Jacqui's father drank in there and Jacqui's father was a weightlifter, the sort of man who would stop trouble by parting the protagonists and single-handedly slinging them through the door, one after the other, where it could carry on outside, which it did, until they got to the stage where they would give in and revert – following a knockout or a submission – to hugging each other like brothers. A small crowd would watch and wait until the traditional words that end fighting were issued.

'I tell thee something, right, thee and me, right, we go back, right, and I'll tell thee something else for nowt: we'll always be *best fuckin' mates*, thee and me. Nothin' – *nothin'* – can *ever* change that: I fuckinloveyoumate.'

Back in the public bar there would be familiar faces getting lashed, and a few frames of pool to be had. But just look at the state of them. I was so ahead of this world by now it was unbelievable. Did I really *originate* from this place? I didn't just drink – so ordinary, so mundane, so commonplace – I took fucking drugs, man!

A year or so after these repellent thoughts had crossed my stoned mind, I got to hear that the whole estate was rife with dope; worse – hard drugs were established too. I had seldom found an idea so depressing. It was not that I'd had my exclusivity as the sole member of the ex-Stoke-on-Trent-dweller's dope-smoking society eclipsed. It was not that at all. It was this: dope-smoking was an act that took place in a plush Victorian house where everybody was totally together, or at the Hammersmith Palais on a Friday night, or outside a pub down by the River Thames in Putney. Dope was meant as an enhancement to a chilled-out lifestyle, not as an escape from the despair that surrounds you and in which you live. Next thing you know you'll have a generation of kids coming up whose parents are drug dealers. This true thought never crossed my mind. It wasn't that I was too zonked to experience a cogent moment like that (because, of course, I was having all my bcst [rubbish] ideas while I was out of it); it wasn't that, it was this: my sights had begun to shift away from Stoke altogether. It had gone beyond the sense of my departing self, where I might consider the place a shit hole but still home. My sense now was that the city was no longer relevant to my life at all. One could speculate that this point of view was influenced by the imports from the West Coast, and that *may* have had something to do with it, but I feel sure I'd have arrived at the opinion regardless.

(Setting this existential moment to one side for a second, it is difficult to overstate the physical poverty of the city. Some years later I was talking to a member of the Socialist Workers Party, a middle-class boy from Norwich. He had been on the 1986 People's March for Jobs, which was a re-enactment of the Jarrow Crusade, organised as a means of celebrating the fiftieth anniversary of that event and at the same time acting as a protest against the high unemployment levels of the day. I mentioned to the SWP boy that I was from Stoke. His face fell. 'Oh dear,' he said. He turned even more serious and earnest than he had been just a second earlier. 'I passed through there on the March,' he said. His lip trembled. 'What a terrible, terrible place. It's just so...' (he struggled for the *mot juste*) '...it's just so utterly *bleak*.' I felt moved to put my hand on his shoulder, to comfort him at the memory of his awful experience.)

The single reason that remained for my return visits was my desire to see my girlfriend.

As soon as she had finished sixth form, Jacqui came down to live with me in London. This would be about six months after I'd latched up with the Blond, who I had brought up to Stoke once or twice, to give him the idea, and to meet my own family. They liked him, albeit that he came from another planet with his pie-in-the-sky ideas about making money and being a great success in life.

My London-savvy had grown. By picking up early editions of the *Evening Standard*, and by being polite to that noxious breed who work in letting agencies – the type who distribute their favours like Bulgarian Commissars – I had managed to rent a more salubrious flat for Jacqui than my erstwhile purple room. Finding accommodation in the capital was more difficult than finding work, a genuine inversion of the situation in my birthplace. The more salubrious pad was a studio flat at the top of a five-storey terrace that had steep steps with wrought-iron hand railings leading to the front door. It was in Cambridge Gardens, a tree-lined thoroughfare off Ladbroke Grove, just north of the tube station. It wasn't until I turned the final flight of the internal staircase in this house that I even knew what a studio flat meant. It meant one room that doubled as both bedroom and living room, with the addition of a tiny kitchen and a tiny bathroom. It didn't add up to all that much in the way of square feet; if you stood back and looked at it dispassionately, what you were paying a fat wad for was one half of a Victorian attic. Still there *were* three rooms, two hundred per cent more rooms than I had been used to. The main sleeping and living area was tight, but there was a skylight set in a sloping ceiling clad with pine slats. The slats gave a Scandinavian feel, the skylight the impression of light and space. An attractive woman of about forty, who looked like Brigitte Bardot and who lived on the ground floor, showed me round. It was a substantial upgrade, and it was nice. I paid the month's deposit and the month's rent in advance immediately to secure the lease, without Jacqui even being there.

'Your girlfriend should see it first,' the woman said.

'Not necessary,' I replied.

'It might be a bit small, for two,' she said.

'No,' I said, 'it'll be fine.'

Though Jacqui had yet to arrive in the city, I lied and said she was already in town and busy at work, as the dent the rent made in my own wages (which I could only prove at £50 a week on the official side) meant I had to pretend that we were a two-income family. Jacqui and I did not last long together in London. The studio flat was fine; it was fun, like caravanning, and she found office work easily, but she had not reached the conclusion that I had regarding the estate where the Elephant was located, nor the wider Potteries beyond. She yearned for Saturday nights with her family, cheese and pineapple and black pudding on cocktail sticks, and, most especially, the company of her parents and her sisters, who she missed desperately. She pined for her home, to which she soon returned; our split would have happened anyway, maybe, but the fact that I had adopted the role of *flâneur*, being seen out and about after hours with out-of-work actresses (waitresses) and other exotic trollops (dishwashers) didn't help. I was already too far gone down the road of change. Jacqui didn't even smoke cigarettes, so there was no way she could join in with the dope. She thought I thought I was someone. And she was right.

There were painful phone calls back and forth, emergency dashes to Stoke and more than several last kisses. There was even an occasion when she returned for a trial reunion. But she had found another boy by then, back in the north. Our trial reunion lasted one night. It was hopeless; it was best for both of us that the whole thing was knocked on the head. I may have behaved in a reprehensible way, but I still had enough about me to feel shame over it all, and I shed tears. In private.

Certainly I would not talk about my ex in derogatory terms, like some did; the Blond's mother, for instance.

The Blond's mother was a formidable person, and a formidable presence. Gwyneth Dunwoody (whose grandmothers were both suffragettes) once made the disparaging observation of her New Labour parliamentary colleague Harriet Harman that Harman was 'one of those women who are of the opinion that they have a God-given right to be amongst the chosen'. The Blond's mother had something of this about her.

The Blond referred to his mother as 'the old dear', which I found patronising and rude, though I believe he meant it affectionately; in Stoke people only called their mum 'mum'. The old dear had an elite squad of girlfriends who turned up and downed spritzers before 'popping out to lunch'. Each of the girlfriends went by a nickname. They divided into two main groups: the wild-eyed sexual predators with single-syllable male monikers like Sid or Frank, and the horse-mad posse straight out of the *Fifth Form at Malory Towers*, the Bunchys and the Scrunchys. The old dear was somewhere in between these two groups and was known as Billie.

'You're better off without her, darling,' Billie advised me, on hearing of our separation and of Jacqui's departure.

Maybe, but not only was it none of Billie's business, it was not her place to discuss her views on the matter with *me* either. I should have told her where to stick it. But of course, my curiosity got the better of me. What was this assessment supposed to mean? Why was I better off without her?

'She was holding you back.'

'Oh really, how?'

'Her attitudes were rather *provincial*, darling. You're better than that.'

You have to laugh, but all the same, what a liberty. I mean, how dare she? Can't she see how her analysis constitutes a damning indictment of *my first love*? And our relationship was only over because it was over, my erstwhile lover hadn't done anything morally wrong, like conducting an affair with a married man or suchlike.

I looked at Billie. It's fair to say she had dumbfounded me with her frank evaluation. But of course, she had softened the blow with flattery: I was *better* than that. Billie was rather good-looking in the way the forty-year-old Virginia Wade was rather good-looking. She exuded an overwhelming air of social ease, she was entirely comfortable in her milieu of old dowagers and ex-debs, and was evidently endowed with the patrician right to say whatever she pleased to the likes of me. She brushed up well and dressed with formal rigour; a two-piece, a Liberty scarf, pearls and maybe a brooch. I never saw her in jeans: that would have been unthinkable. She was the first person I ever encountered who owned an en-suite bathroom, which was her inner sanctum and which contained very many shelves, dressers and mirrors, and very many unctions. Bathing went on for extended periods in there. There was a hint of the Roman Empire about the length of time given over to preparations before one was fit to face one's people. Billie's vocal sounds were completely tortured; she had taken received pronunciation into that realm where, for practical purposes, it's a different language, where a house is a hice, an awful cresh is what happens when hice prices fall, and one can never be merely angry, one must always be absllivi, as in, absolutely livid.

The everyday expression of greeting, 'Darling! How lovely to see you', comes out in one single high-pitched multi-syllable: *Darholseyooo!*

Despite all of these shortcomings, I liked Billie, a feeling I gathered was reciprocal. I respected her fighting qualities; in common with my own mother she was a single woman who looked out for her family. She worked in a wallpaper shop in the Fulham Road, not exactly B&Q, rather the kind of emporium that has the fuck-off attitude of a Bond Street art dealer, the kind that sells rolls of Osborne and Little at £30 a go. I knew a small amount about wallpaper on account of my father's work. (I was more or less out of touch with him, as I had been ever since the divorce. We might speak on the phone once a year; I might see him for a drink at Christmas. That was it.) You could paper a whole room for thirty quid if you went in for a few rolls of the basic stuff, and still have change left over for the paste and sundries. I knew enough to know that. *Your house was very small, with woodchip on the wall,* as Jarvis Cocker would sing years later, describing the *mise-en-scène* of a sticky romance that took place in the parlour of a typical terraced house in Sheffield. Billie would have allowed woodchip across her threshold as soon as commission an Artexer to ice the ceiling of her boudoir in the style of peaked-up snow on a Christmas cake.

Taste was key to Billie. It was *taste* that constituted her principles. She would have become a suffragette only if it involved a protest against the installation of double-glazed plastic replacement windows, or stone cladding. I pictured her chaining herself to her wrought-iron railings to prevent such a monstrous affront from taking place.

Her Osborne and Little papers came in muted pastel stripes or subtle motifs of fleur-de-lys. There was no place for wood-chip here, wall and ceiling finishes could only be flat, suggestions of interior texture came about through fabric and textiles. Decorative matters could provoke discussion that went on for hours. There were no books in Billie's house, with the exception of coffee-table volumes about antiques and furniture. The only other casual reading was a large pile of backdated copies of *World of Interiors*, the bible of doing places up. Billie's decorative modes were certainly not derived from the Bauhaus, a movement of which she would never have heard, but her codes of decoration were almost as rigid; they certainly came from *somewhere*, and they almost constituted a movement. Like Modernism, and it's manifestation in art, Abstract Expressionism, furnishings and decorations in her world could only be put together from an agreed limited palette sanctioned by a specific clique of elevated individuals. In this case the limited palette was derived from those interior design shops of the Fulham and Kings Roads where she and her clan worked and hung out. The Metropolitan Museum of Modern Art of this subculture was Peter Jones, the John Lewis flagship store that gazes out over Sloane Square through its famous curtain walling. The only criticism I ever heard made of Peter Jones was that sometimes, perhaps, it could be a little staid, but otherwise it always 'got it right'. Getting things right was key. The sighting of the tiniest little incorrect signifier – say a paper lampshade from Habitat – would say *everything* about you. It would say everything wrong about you.

Unlike Abstract Expressionism, the aim of which was to protect pure painting as the prime artistic activity by drawing attention to the *ineluctable flatness of the canvas* (this is what the advocates of Jackson Pollock and Mark Rothko would claim, anyway), it was my sense that the motivations of the SW6 Interior Designer Movement did not spring from the same kind of philosophical and intellectual stance. It was my sense instead that their agreed code derived from a slightly different instinct, namely fat profit. Their decorative cartel constituted an agreement on what it was, exactly, that could enable a lady to charge herself out at the maximum possible rate. The trick they used in promoting themselves as 'interior designers' (when what they actually did was work in shops) was to imply to a client that their *gift* of a divine sense of aesthetics would ultimately enable a property to *sell at a premium*. The movement's guiding principle was in hiking hice prices ever upwards in order to satisfy life's principal ambition: to make as much money as possible from one's property before moving on to the next up-and-coming arca in order to repeat the exercise quickly, before everyone else caught on. A key part of this game was the renaming of areas. Some years later Billie moved out of the street off the Fulham Palace Road (aka: *Bishops Park*) down to a scruffy road just off the Wandsworth one-way system. It was no time at all before Billie was baffling her new neighbours by repeatedly referring to something called 'The Harbour Triangle' which, it finally transpired, was the area in which the neighbours themselves had been living for generations without ever having heard of its proper title.

The Blond and I would sometimes visit Billie's wallpaper emporium. We fixed our rotas to do a late followed by an early, which meant that we worked a day on, a day off. We synchronised as much as possible so that our free time coincided. We would hang about Billie's shop to see if anything might fall our way in terms of lunch. On a quiet day we might be taken down to Tootsies, a *fabulous* hamburger place on Parson's Green. Once I was on terms with the other shop girls, and the owner of the place – had performed my turn by saying 'book' and 'bath' – things were fine. They got over themselves enough to speak to me normally without having to keep up their own act of being too posh (because they worked in a posh shop) to notice me. Of course they couldn't really be all that posh, could they? Otherwise, what were they doing working for a living in the first place? That was the way I saw it, though it does not, in fact, always follow; the young Lady Diana Spencer lived in a mansion block just round the corner from my first bedsit off Earl's Court Road. I would routinely see the press pack loitering round the door of the block first thing in the morning, waiting for her to appear on her way to work, which was in a kindergarten. Interior design shops and kindergartens offer 'deb jobs' for girls who are filling in time while they wait for their prince charming to happen along.

There were certain customers that only Billie, the self-appointed shop manager, dealt with. I watched as the victims were conducted through the process of selection, Billie skilfully guiding them up through the sample books and swatches. Choosing a wallpaper was the same as selecting a dish from a menu; it required similar reassurances from the expert, the confirmation and affirmation to the client that their instincts were broadly correct, but that there were other better (more expensive) options available too. Waiters did the same at the hotel, where the ten percent service charge actually *did* accrue in the pay packet: it was therefore in the best interests of the staff to recommend the most expensive wines and champagnes on the list. We all worked in the service sector, in jobs that demanded a measure of role play and performance: it was this that we shared in common. I was much more polite at work than I was in real life, similarly the Blond was required to behave with unnatural deference, and here we were now, observing Billie in action. The thing in her case, though, was that she was *more* like herself than usual: more authoritative, with additional top-end modulation on the voice-screech, in order to let the client know who was boss. She was confident; this was her world and she ruled it. I took notes.

Billie ran her own interiors business on the side. Here was a well-conceived scheme, given that the day job introduced her to a steady stream of potential income. Through this channel, I dipped my toe into new waters insofar as 'doing a foreigner' went.

I had already been putting in overtime, working shifts for an outside catering agency based in Kensington High Street. The jobs involved waiting at parties in private houses. It was well paid, and took me to parts of London that I wouldn't otherwise see. In a small house in Richmond, an anxious pink woman employed me to serve champagne at a 'drinks and nibbles' do that was attended by David Attenborough. Though I had heard of him, he meant nothing to me, but he was evidently big in Richmond. I had never seen so many ladies fawn over one very ordinary-looking man in a V-neck jumper. I asked someone what, exactly, he did. The answer was that he presented wildlife programmes for the BBC. Stone the crows.

Another assignment required three staff, so I acted as sub-agent by pulling in a couple of others from the hotel. We headed north to a destination called Stanmore, which is the final stop at the far end of the Jubilee line. It was my first (and last) overland tube ride into suburbia. I had never been there before, where wide green commons spread out in front of spacious wide streets, where lions stood on gateposts in front of fake Edwardian houses with fake leaded windows. Or were they even real Edwardian houses? I couldn't quite tell. Our client lived in one of these. Inside, it was decorated in the style of the baroque nouveau riche. I don't know whether I had heard of that expression then, but you don't have to be familiar with the French for ostentatious vulgarity in order to be able to recognise and disparage it. As with the later excesses of Thatcher's kids – that gruesome generation of Porsche-snorting strivers coining it in the City – it appeared that I was genetically predisposed to sneer at any personification or emblem of new money. Perhaps I am a natural-born snob. Perhaps inverted snobbery is just the disguise I use for it.

Our hostess was a short, overweight, panicky, kaftan-wearing late-thirty-something mess. She was throwing a surprise fortieth birthday party for her husband, who was the manager of Status Quo or whoever. A white grand piano stood as the centrepiece of the lounge but it didn't fit, being too big for the room. My two waiter friends worked from a bar furnished with cocktail shakers and optics in the corner of this crooner's lounge while I circulated with canapés. The bar wasn't set up specially for this event; it was a fixture.

The guests were a bunch of freeloaders.

'O, another drink barman, please,' they were saying in put-on la-di-da voices, as if we were some sort of joke. The freeloaders were versions of the fat men with cigars from the country pubs of south Cheshire, but with considerably worse manners.

The real purpose of our presence here was one-upmanship: we were just another trinket, a vainglorious accessory to the kaftan-wearer's considerably-richer-than-you, petit-bourgeoisie, grand piano lifestyle.

When the husband arrived home it was clear that the unexpected party of piss-artists was his idea of a rotten surprise. He was a good-looking, louche man dressed in the uniform of the aging rocker: denims, pinstripe suit jacket, crumpled shirt, collar-length hair, split ends. It was obvious at a glance that he would be having numerous affairs with the spare groupies from Status Quo or whoever, and had probably fucked the wives of half of the freeloaders there too. Mrs Rocker was desperate that he still be in love with her. This, too, was obvious, as was the fact that he wasn't: I had seen enough of divorce to recognise what was what on that score. I would like to say that I felt sympathy for the woman, but I couldn't because her neediness was expressed by making a show of herself, by loudness; I could easily imagine her having a fight on the front hardstanding with one of the freeloaders later on. I loathe loudness. Women who bawl their kids out in the supermarket make me shudder; families of fatties wobbling down the seafront at Great Yarmouth on a bank holiday Monday (I took Mother there once), all yelling at each other in unison while spreading a litter of fish-and-chip wrappings in their wake, make me think that selective mass genocide would be an excellent idea.

'I can get my own drink. Thanks.'

Here was the husband advising us that he wished we weren't there, and letting us know that the last thing he required in his own home was staff to serve him his brandy and Coke.

I knew how he felt. I woke up one morning after a sleepover at the Blond's, went downstairs to put the kettle on, and encountered a strange woman, dusting. It took me a second to work out what was going on. The only experience I'd had of cleaners up to that moment were the mums of some of my friends back home who did part-time jobs in hospitals and schools. What was it with these people? Was it beneath them to clean up their own mess? I was outraged. I offered the cleaner a cup of tea, which she meekly declined. Years later, I attended the wedding of a mate, a public-school drop-out plumber. He was getting hitched to a girl who was heir to a high-street butcher's empire. The service took place at a church in a village that the butchering family owned, near Bath. I had an eighteen-month-old son, Jack, by then. Jack began wailing as soon as the Wedding March started, so I took him outside to play amongst the gravestones while they got on with it. There was a wall around the churchyard. The villagers were ranged along this wall, watching and waiting. Jack toddled down their way, so I said a few hellos, and words to explain why we were outside: 'He doesn't like weddings, he knows it can only end in tears,' etc. Not a single one of them said a word back. Mutes? No. It slowly dawned on me what the situation was: same as with the cleaner, if I was connected to the wedding party, we were too elevated to dare to talk to. This time I wasn't outraged; I was appalled: I didn't know we still had the feudal system.

So: I don't employ a cleaner. I just can't do it. I'm one of the few people in my circle who does his own dishes, uses his own vacuum cleaner and knows how the washing machine works.

Fuck Mr Rocker and his bad attitude to being served a drink, anyway.

I went for a piss. The bathroom had a marble floor and taps in the form of dolphins. I smoked a cigarette. Not done on duty, unprofessional. But I would never see these people again, so: so what. I stubbed my Camel butt in an onyx ashtray.

By the end of the evening we had gone overtime and were due double rate for hours worked after eleven, plus the cab fee back into central London as the tube station at Stanmore would be shut. Mrs Rocker argued the facts and figures of the bill for an age before she finally got her purse out, still refusing to cough up the full amount. No wonder her husband had so many women on the side. We took what we could get off her, and I stole the onyx ashtray as a means of settling the balance. We were later accused of this crime, but as my previous record with the catering agency was squeaky clean, the matter was interpreted as one of those cases that occasionally came their way; a bad-apple client trying to get out of paying the agency fees. It was Mrs Rocker's word against mine, and it was me they trusted. The item in question would never be found, that was for sure, as I had smashed it into a wheelie bin under the Ladbroke Grove flyover on my way home as an objection against its aesthetic offence and all that it stood for.

I let myself back into our studio flat. The whole place was less than half the size of the kitchen in Stanmore. Here I was working until past midnight on top of the day job, having to negotiate with charlatans simply to get what I was rightfully owed, and being used as a token of nouveau richeness, and still I was only earning buttons. I was on the wrong track.

But I really *didn't* have any ambition to make money. I wasn't just saying it when I said it; I meant it. Not that it would have changed my circumstances much even if I was on a grand a week: the truth of the matter was that I was useless with cash and spent the stuff as fast as I could earn it. Whatever was left after rent was taken care of went on carefully selected dandy accessories to go with the Italian overcoat: vintage Tootal polka-dot silk scarves, two-tone winkle-pickers, thin woollen ties and so on. My appearance was of paramount importance to me – and why shouldn't it be? – appearance was the snap criteria by which I judged everybody else.

The single fact that allowed me to see some of my fellow employees in a more neutral light, and not to spring so readily to these shallow evaluations in my workplace, was that we all wore uniform. You were responsible for acquiring your own white shirts, bow ties and black trousers, as well as footwear, which afforded ample scope for customising the basic kit. My shirts were Ben Sherman button-downs, for instance, though I was one of a very few people in the whole place who appreciated this key sartorial detail. It was, then, only the jackets that were supplied by the hotel. They came in a tint of beige the colour of cold gruel, and in several cuts, very few of which fitted any normal human being. You sent them away to be laundered once a week, and picked up a couple of clean ones at the same time. I was always first in the queue for this, so that I could choose two single-breasted cotton jackets in something near to my size and not two

double-breasted monstrosities manufactured out of rayon and
built to swathe a hippo.

Any cash I had left after blowing my dough on clothes went
on records, the pub, dope, eating out and on bills associated with
keeping the Mini on the road.

I would never get rich in catering, anyway. The Blond told me
as much himself.

'Gotagetoutofitmateseriously.'

It was his habit to string his words together, as if speaking as
fast as possible somehow added to the gravitas of what was being said. But he was a boy in a hurry in any event: he was going
to be a millionaire before he was thirty, a fact he would repeat
at regular intervals, and an ambition he would illustrate in his
personal conduct. The weekend building-trade work that we began to do through the good offices of Billie was straightforward
enough, semi-skilled manual labour. We would take doors to be
dipped and stripped by immersion into a tank of acid. When
they had dried out, we would return them to their hinges and
finish them by waxing with wire wool and buffing with rags. Because we used Billie's hatchback for the transport (a silver Fiesta
XR2i) the Blond split the money 60:40 in his favour. The reason
that I received less for my (equal) part in the work was that he
was charging an agent's fee for supplying both the jobs and the
wheels (his mother's). In my view this was anti-friendly. I would
never dream, for instance, of charging him a percentage of the
expenses that went into the Mini, which were not inconsider-
able, and which were invested in the service of enabling the pair
of us to run round all night long to various parties, pubs and
other venues, several of which were thirty miles away in some
village called Guildford. When I suggested that, by extending
his principles to their logical conclusion, he might care to cough
up for a share of my petrol, tax, tyres and insurance costs, he
laughed in a deeply ironic manner. This was *completely* different

from him taking a cut out of me, and as a matter of fact I was being a propertightwadgitnorthenflatcapgit even to suggest it. Did I keep a whippet in the boot too, or what?

*****

One day I saved the Blond's life.

Living at home excused him from the requirement to pay rent, and since he didn't know the first thing about fashion (being safely and routinely clad head to toe in denim), he invested his pay packets in slightly different ways from me. He became the first person I knew to own a Sony Walkman. During a shift change, when he was finishing his early and I was beginning my late, we talked over the form. I was to be working on my own in room service that night: he reported that the place had been as dead as a doornail all day (as well as the routine quietness of a Saturday evening when all guests were out at the theatre, we experienced these occasional flat spots) so there'd be absolutely nothing to do at all unless I fancied letting myself in and out of empty rooms to top up inkwells and change the blotting paper on the writing mats. This dreary outlook enabled me, after a considerable amount of begging and cajoling, to persuade the Blond to loan me the Walkman. It is difficult to exaggerate just how thrilling the novelty of the personal stereo was at the beginning. Its introduction coincided with the birth of a new imported fitness lifestyle activity called jogging that had arrived from America. Jogging enabled you to run round Hyde Park; the addition of a Walkman let you do it with punk rock blasting into your head. In this way, you could set up violent clashes of word and image. The sound of Stiff Little Fingers howling *Get an alternative Ulster, be an anti-security force* would be thundering into your eardrum while a glance to your left showed the Royal Standard flying over Buckingham Palace and head-on you had to step aside with some zip in order to avoid being run down by the Household Cavalry.

The Blond was in the habit of rolling the volume-dial up to ten as he listened to U2 while cycling to work and back. On this day, the day that I borrowed the Walkman, he was knocked off his bike by a London bus on his way home. He spent a week in intensive care and some more days on the very poorly list in the Royal Brompton Hospital on Fulham Road. He suffered cracked ribs, a broken arm, a punctured lung and plenty in the way of cuts and bruises. It was his rock chick sister who told me the news, by landline, a whole day later (it seems an extraordinary delay, post-mobile phone). I went to visit him even before his mother, who was on holiday in Sun City, South Africa. (I had to overlook that completely. Apartheid was at its peak, all matters white South African were boycotted by everybody, even by people who didn't have any principles whatsoever.) It upset me a lot to see my friend connected to tubes. Notwithstanding his fiscal tightness, by now I regarded him as my best mate. We both considered that it was the lending of the Walkman that saved his life because we both knew that riding along London's roads without the benefit of all your senses was a real danger. I too had nearly met my maker at half-six one Sunday morning when (once again) a bus driver (cyclists are beneath their line of vision) didn't see me and forced me into the centre of Marble Arch. I could feel the blast of heat from the exhaust as he came within an inch of smashing into me after he had flown blithely out of the bottom of the Edgware Road. The absence of the Walkman afforded the Blond that same split second I'd had to swerve and avoid a full impact. This was how we saw it. I'd helped him out financially too, by enabling him to get an action going against London Transport. The very first words he wrote down on my visit (he could not talk because of the breathing tubes) were, 'I'm going to sue the bastards.'

At least he had some hope of achieving that aim without the defence team being able to cite 'Mr Bono singing into the claimant's earholes' as significant contributory negligence.

This scrape with mortality decided the Blond on a new path in life. He quit the hotel and resolved to travel for a few months in Europe. I copied him, led on (as he was) by the three actresses (chambermaids) that we were chasing.

We had both split up with our first serious girlfriends, and I had become a lothario. As everyone had to have a nickname, mine became Julio, after the Spanish crooner, Iglesias. At a certain point I was running three girls at the same time. The attractive blonde woman from the ground floor, Brigitte Bardot, the one who had shown me the studio flat in the first place, had come on to me one night soon after Jacqui left. She was forty and, underneath her housecoat, was wearing the traditional seduction kit of stockings and suspenders. This was a wet dream come true for a young man like me. Her flesh felt completely different to that of a nineteen-year-old's, which was all I had known until then. It was soft, and moved slightly on her frame; it felt, of course, much more mature, but she had a youthful enough appetite for being at it all night long, and demanded clitoral satisfaction as insistently as any feminist. In addition to Brigitte, I had a posh girl who worked in Asprey's, the Bond Street jewellers, by day, and then came over to do part-time dishwashing in the hotel by night, in order to pay off some 'horrific debts' she'd run up on Daddy's account. She ambushed me, dragged me up against the sink in a pantry one evening and fucked me there and then (I was skinny and Mowgli-like, which enabled me to be taken like that. In addition to my exotic pronunciations of 'book' and 'bath', the physical attributes of an urchin seemed enough to make me exotic and desirable to certain women.) The debt-ridden deb lived in a filthy dive, a basement flat in Barons Court, one of Daddy's properties. She only wanted sex: she had no further use for me beyond that, though she was also insistent that I perform frequently and with due vigour. Brigitte turned mad, ambushing me at every turn, wanting to know where I had been, and with whom, even finding out Billie's phone number and calling her up in the middle of the night in a paranoid check on my whereabouts.

'Outrageous, darling. I'm afraid I had to put a flea in her ear.'

Brigitte was talking wedding bells, which meant I had to avoid my own flat now. I parked round the corner and sneaked in and out when I needed to get stuff. Then the Barons Court girl started stalking me. I don't know why, maybe she had been running a double bluff that had failed. Perhaps I *was* actually supposed to fall in love with her and not just take at face value her simple, and to my way of thinking, ideal desire for sex with no strings attached. Being a stud was turning out to be dangerous.

The third girlfriend, the actress-chambermaid, was one of a group of three students who had turned up at the hotel to make beds and fold linen until they had saved up enough cash for their European jaunt, the jaunt that the Blond was joining. The third girlfriend was blonde herself. In fact, so was the posh girl, though she was dirty blonde. I suppose that was how I got away with it: all the hairs on my shoulders matched up. The actress-chambermaid appeared sweet and normal. She lived in Southend-on-Sea, a safe distance from the other two, a bolt-hole, even, though seeing her did involve an eighty-mile round trip up and down the A13 in order to fit in our love life, as well as our occasional visits to the cinema and theatre, to indulge her passion for performance. I had very seldom been to the theatre. The only play I really remembered seeing was a local piece of agitprop about the closing of the Shelton Bar steelworks in Stoke, which wasn't so much theatre as politics. I found, and I still find, theatre to be a dubious activity peopled by dubious persons. The further

Something to Be

I went down the alternative route, the greater were the chances that I'd find myself watching some interminable two-hand dirge performed in a room above a pub on Shepherd's Bush Green or on Upper Street, Islington, enduring the performance of a play dealing with *issues*. These rooms-above-pubs seemed designed to upset my equilibrium, peopled as they were by gangs of pseuds who genuinely *did* think they were somebody simply because they were all wearing turtleneck sweaters, stiff denims with six-inch turn-ups, second-hand leather jackets and Joe 90 specs.

But back in the Cliffs Pavilion, Southend-on-Sea, I could put up with a tepid gin and tonic served with just the single ice cube, and a few am-dram luvvies; they were simply a part of the price I had to pay for my new life of perpetual screwing: they were game, these southern girls; you couldn't knock that. I deserved my nickname, and in the process of deserving it, I discovered another downside to being a stud, apart from the danger: studs never sleep.

*****

Before we take the Magic Bus down to Athens and leave hotel life behind for ever, there are a pair of other boys who cannot go without mention. The first was a rotund young waiter whose family owned a country pile in a tiny hamlet near Godalming. The rotund boy was 375th in line to the throne, or some such. His neighbours back in Surrey included members of the rock aristocracy. Eric Clapton was one, no doubt Sting would move next door in due course. The rock star country squire was a nauseating concept to a new-wave disciple like me who believed that pop music was an agent for enabling social change. That meant sticking to your principles, not selling out by donning a tweed cap and wellington boots and shooting at pheasants. And Clapton made it considerably worse by slurring some racist comments at a gig as well. Of course, my point of view was wholly irrelevant in the sense that a singer like Clapton would never have shared it in the first place. John Lennon, on the other hand, might have done.

Lennon was in a different frame of reference from Clapton, or from any of the repulsive and redundant ilk of Genesis, Yes and all the rest of the public-schoolboy progressive-rock crowd that punk had so effectively blown away, all of whom deserved only to die. If The Jam and The Clash were my older, sharper brothers, Lennon was a favourite uncle, the one who would take you out for a drink and infest your head with brilliant, revolutionary and subversive ideas, ideas designed to make you believe that the world was yours for the taking. Lennon had views, morals; he had a stance and a position. He was shot by Mark Chapman, an individual who was far enough gone to act out for real the fate that I believed Clapton and his like deserved. Of course, when you say that people deserve to die, you are playing fast and loose with rhetoric; you don't actually mean it. For Chapman, Lennon was worse than any of those dinosaurs because he sang 'Imagine', yet lived the lifestyle of the super-rich. Lennon was a phony. Phony is a key word, phoniness a key concept, in *The Catcher in the Rye*, the bible for the disaffected young male. Chapman had a copy of Salinger's paperback in his pocket when he unloaded his .38 revolver into Lennon's back. I wondered if he also owned the 45rpm single of 'Imagine'. I assumed he must have. The b-side of 'Imagine' is 'Working-Class Hero', a song I used to play repeatedly when I was still at home.

As soon as you're born they make you feel small,
by giving you no time instead of it all,
till the pain is so big you feel nothing at all;
a working-class hero is something to be,
a working-class hero is something to be.

Something to Be

Some would argue that this was as phony as 'Imagine', what with Lennon being a middle-class boy himself. Not me: you can't come from Liverpool and be middle class: this was my view. It's a compelling lyric, ideally pitched to whip a young man into a frenzy of self-pity. Actually, I was given plenty of time, as far as I could tell, but you would never catch me acknowledging that because I was much more interested in identifying with Lennon's pain. I knew exactly what he meant. He was writing the second chapter to Larkin's 'This Be The Verse'; what he meant was: they fuck you up, the outside world, the rulers with their stupid rules, they mean to do it, and they do.

One way or another, the working classes are trampled underfoot and suppressed by exactly the kind of people who live here, in Godalming. These must be Lennon's 'folks on the hill', I thought, as I drove the Mini down a half-mile drive of sparkling gravel to visit HRH the Rotund's family seat.

First you must learn how to smile as you kill, if you want to be like the folks on the hill.

I ought to have despised the whole set-up and planted an incendiary device in the conservatory to do my bit for the class war. But I neither despised nor planted. Here was what I was repeatedly discovering – once I had left my bedroom in the Potteries and my record player behind me, the rest of the world did not always turn out as advertised; not only did it fail to square with the polemic used to describe it, the parts that were supposed to be so disgusting often turned out to be rather charming, or at least fascinating.

The rotund boy was a hapless case, the loser (by dint of going into catering) of a hapless family. What one discovered at the end of the gravel driveway that led to the ancestral home was the gentry fallen on hard times. The mother was swilling gin day and night because the father had done a runner with an au pair some years earlier. The father's despicable act was attributed to being driven to madness by taxation under Labour in the seventies: his behaviour was Jim Callaghan's fault, rather than the consequence of lust.

Whatever the father's motivations, his departure had brought shame and more debt on the family, and his name was never to be mentioned. A fleet of sisters just about kept the mansion afloat by offering riding lessons and pursuing ridiculous business ideas like practising as (unqualified) vets, concocting flower arrangements from the hedgerow and making bird tables and dreamcatchers to sell at fêtes. I had gone down there to work for the weekend on the latest of these wheezes, catering for wedding parties. A marquee had been erected on the lawn and a hundred guests were due to arrive. In between setting cutlery and carrying glasses, I nosed about the place. Even though it was a nice day outside, it was cold indoors. A pair of old terriers occupied a damask sofa with stuffing spilling out. The rugs were threadbare and stained with patches that were, in all likelihood, dog piss. On the walls framed pictures were set at skewed angles; those that weren't paintings of horses were photographs of the children riding in gymkhana events. There was also a not-very-lifelike oil portrait of HRH the Rotund. I wouldn't have had that on my wall, if it had been me. I studied a photograph of him taking a fence on a horse. He had been a rotund teenager too, I noted; it looked harsh on the animal, being required to take off under that handicap. Gymkhana. This was the first time I'd ever known anyone involved in such an activity. The only thing I knew about horses was nothing – I had an annual bet on the Grand National and the Derby and that was that. This is a matter that has changed; a lot. Days after I received my first decent royalty cheque, I made a snap decision to give myself the afternoon off. I drove to Great Yarmouth racecourse, not far from where I live now in Norwich. After the third race, I returned to the parade ring where I stood and watched the auction following a selling plate. The winning horse went for 7,200 guineas. My cheque would cover that and leave a bit over. I immediately began to wonder if the balance would stretch to training fees.

They're not exactly the aristocracy, though, the horses that go under the hammer at Great Yarmouth. Racehorses are all about bloodlines, of course. Those that run at Yarmouth often have the pedigree equivalence of an onyx ashtray in Stanmore. Further up the divisions they are more like the crumbling pile in Godalming, and the best, those that go for hundreds of thousands of guineas, belong to the super-rich back at Claridge's and the Connaught. And even they are subject to value judgements based on class.

'Of course, racing's not what it used to be – it's all Arabs now.'

It was Billie who had advised me of this back in Fulham as she prevaricated between Hermes scarves and dabbed her neck with Chanel No. 5 while preparing to shoot off down to Ascot one morning.

'Still, they might be able to buy livestock, but they can't buy *class*. Are my seams straight, darling?'

You can't buy class. I liked that. I used to use it as a joke, an in-joke, one that I could direct at myself. I'd be throwing up under Hammersmith Bridge after eight pints. 'You can't buy class, Foster,' I'd say to my pissed-up alter ego. 'You've either got it or you haven't, lad.'

If you can't buy it, then, perhaps what you have to do is barter it. Otherwise, one will always remain fixed in the class in which one began; it will be a matter, like livestock, that is entirely fixed by bloodline, that one is powerless to change. And this cannot be the case, otherwise my old school friends would not have been able to accuse me of being middle class.

I took one last glance around the shabby lounge. The reading matter was bizarre: on a low table there were copies of the *Horse and Hound* and *Country Living*. The single book was *Debrett's*

Guide to the Season. I needed something for later: I always read myself to sleep, but there was nothing for me there. Someone was calling me to help out with the salads.

Back in the kitchen it was chaos. I tried to be hygienic in my work (I had learned my trade this way), but given the general condition of the fixtures and fittings it was not easy. Chipped Belfast sinks and blackened timber draining boards were the order of the day. The standard of cleanliness would not have earned a Health and Safety certificate, not even in 1981. I was shaking water off lettuce leaves, trying not to touch anything, when suddenly a row erupted. I don't know what it was about, but my colleague was got at by his mother; picked on. Ghosts flew out of the closet. She thought he had tried to contact his father, something like that. I always felt slightly sorry for him because he was an awkward boy. As well as being overweight, he was one of those sexless cases, probably not gay, but never going to sleep with a girl either. There were one or two of them at work, particularly on the front-of-house side. There is something about the fastidiousness of waiting-on and the cold distance of reception duties that suits an asexual disposition. This meant that HRH was excluded from general conversations about fucking. As well as that, he didn't drink, apart from being addicted to gallons of apple juice. This excluded him from drunken japes. But for all that we lacked in common, I liked His Highness, he was harmless and decent and I counted him as a friend. Even though they were my principal hobbies, sex and drinking were rather impoverished means by which to judge someone. I knew that, and so I was able to feel proud of myself that I could rise above applying my usual standards in his case, even if it amounted to only a slight sense of pride, of no real value. I remembered feeling like this once before, at school, when I did not participate in the bullying of a pair of slightly unworldly mixed-race twins that were the butt of many of the bad things that went on in the playground. I did nothing, but I did nothing to intervene either. There's no pride in that.

It was by my clothes and by my status as a car owner that I generated such personal kudos as I had. And by my conquests. Sex was my non-cash currency. So I tried it on with His Highness's sister, later on, when we had done working, but she gave me the knock-back. Perhaps it was a straightforward case of not doing one-night stands with her brother's drunken mates, but I wondered if, even though the family were having to go into service to make ends meet, it was not more plainly a matter of me being too common for the rumble in the hay that I had in mind. It was partly the argument in the kitchen that caused me to think this way: she played her full part in it, and it happened as if I was not there. She made no concession to a stranger being present; I was of as much consequence as one of the terriers. But I was simply being paranoid: in this sense, life in Godalming was, in fact, just the same as life in Fegg Hayes – I wasn't sure that I could remember ever visiting a friend's house back home for more than half an hour without some sort of barney erupting in front of my eyes. And so, as I thought the matter through, I could reach this conclusion: people from mansions in Surrey were not so unlike us. This was how, and why, I could quite like them; this was how, and why, it was *okay* to quite like them.

In spite of the recriminating and the gin, HRH's mother maintained certain standards. A bed had been made up in a guest wing, which was a stable. It was even colder there than in the main house, but it was much cleaner, with sparkling white bed linen. Someone had put flowers out in a vase and left a bible on the bedside table. I smoked a joint out of the window. A bible. What in the name of Moses was I supposed to do with that? But on the other hand, perhaps it would make amusing reading while stoned: that was the great thing about dope, it gave you the chance to re-evaluate the comic potential of every single item of cultural production. But, as it turned out, even California's finest export couldn't turn Exodus into the Furry Freak Brothers.

If it was through HRH the Rotund that I learned about, or at least saw in action, the bankrupt gentry, then the second boy I must mention was his friend Liam. It was through Liam that I was brought into close quarters with England's super-elite. Liam was tall and gawky; he came from a council house in the same village as HRH. Liam was effectively a serf to HRH and his family: he had done odd jobs on the estate when he was a kid – that was how they knew each other. And then they had attended the same catering school. The way their relationship worked was that Liam bullied HRH, albeit it ever so gently and in a nice enough way. He dominated him like an older brother, keeping him in his place in the pecking order that *he* had established. Liam was the second-most money-obsessed individual I had ever encountered. But whereas the Blond had expansive plans, Liam modelled himself on Scrooge, constantly counting his change out in piles and squirrelling his savings away. His father had split with his mother, and Liam had obsessively taken on the idea that it was down to him to ensure that adequate financial provision was made for the family.

I had been in London for a year now and I had yet to meet a young male hotel worker whose parents remained together. Perhaps it is the post-divorce domestic void that the young boys step into, that naturally suggests the work. The most prominent of his generation of celebrity chefs, Gordon Ramsay, says that his own absent father, to whom he rarely speaks, said to him that 'cooking is for poufs'. Though my own father was not like that about it, I knew the type. Not only were these fathers fools, all too often they were failures on their own terms too; drunks and gamblers. That's the point, that's why they say the stupid things they say about cooking or other work that is 'unmanly'. Ramsay was nineteen or so when his parents split, and big enough to take it, maybe, or at least big enough for it to contribute to forming his talent, his perfection-neurosis. But the boys I was encountering were all younger at the time of their parents' separation. The fact of the matter is this: it's the father's absence that forces you to grow up fast, that puts you into the position of carrying out domestic tasks that are traditionally associated with the female, in order to back your mother up. The resentment boys feel towards the father for creating these circumstances takes years to fade, if it ever does.

*****

Liam lived in the Savoy Group staff hostel. It's a good address, in a garden square in Holland Park, and consisted of two substantial Victorian houses knocked into one. This created a warren with staircases leading up and down out of improbable doorways, like a haunted house at a funfair. Toast was being made for much of the day, which assisted in suppressing the dominant odour of rancid socks and the much worse odour of rancid chef's whites. I lived there myself, in-between places, for about six weeks. It was the cheapest possible option available on accommodation, though it could involve sharing several to a room, and one day a new person might arrive without any warning and cover the walls with life-size posters of Adam and the Ants while you were out at work. Imagine coming back 'home' to that. This was the point at which I left. Never mind that the new room-mate was probably a serial killer; no way was I prepared to live a life in which the first thing I saw when I opened my eyes in the morning was a New Romantic Pirate throwing a swashbuckling pose.

Liam had no such problems – cheap digs is cheap digs. Liam was committed to work and to work only. He was dedicated to sniffing out extra shifts wherever he could find them, the most common being to provide assistance to the skeleton staff that made up the 'room service nightshift' – which consisted of two Italians covering six floors. You could pick up a couple of extra hours – and decent tips – between 11pm and 1am, working up a sweat as you ran about like a maniac serving nightcaps and toasties to guests as they rolled in from their nights out. After it all went quiet, you could slip the security doorman a couple of bottles of Carlsberg '68, which was all that was required for him to turn a blind eye to whatever it was that you had stuffed under your coat. I don't think Liam ever paid for food or drink as long as he was in the job, as indeed I never paid for a packet of cigarettes. Liam would host party nights back in his room in Holland Park, where bottles of Krug and boxes of twiglets would be served along with packets of fig rolls as supplied by HRH, these being his biscuit of choice. They were totally male affairs, these soirées, during which, once they were hammered on vintage champagne, Adam and the Ants fans would amuse themselves by setting fire to the hairs on their legs using jet sprays of lighter fuel. Adam and the Ants were a mystery to Liam. He was one of those odd people who have no knowledge whatsoever of music. If you asked him what sort of thing he liked, he would pause and try to remember a singer's name. Frank Sinatra, he would reply.

Liam's mother was a housekeeper, at Eton. The Mini was pressed into service for a trip down there to meet her.

All that I knew about Eton was its name and a narrative account of certain events that I had learned from The Jam. 'Eton Rifles' comprises a lyric that describes a confrontation between a Right to Work and a gang of public schoolboys, from the point of view of the marchers:

We were no match for their untamed wit,
though some of the lads said they'd be back next week.

Twenty miles west of Holland Park, we pulled up outside the

alma mater of England's ruling class. I thought it an odd building, perhaps what a church might look like if it were really a prison. The architecture was not the thing though, the boys were the thing; they zipped about as if their pants were on fire. Kitted out in an archaic uniform of bumfreezer jackets or tailcoats, together with stick-up collars with white ties, Etonian scholars had only one speed: fast. An identikit battalion of Billy Whizz-influenced Hugh Grants, their mission was plain – to get to wherever it was they were going by yesterday.

All that rugby puts hairs on your chest,
what chance have you got against a tie and a crest.

In common with the author of 'Eton Rifles', I hated them on sight.

Inside the quad, the architecture seemed to soften, it became beautiful, it was the dreaming spires from a poem I could vaguely remember. And it was something you could never have if you were me or anyone like me. You could only experience this schooling through an accident of birth. Nothing could be more unfair.

Liam's mum was the embodiment of matronliness; bonny, authoritative, in charge. The boys, in archetypal public-schoolboy fashion, clearly adored their 'Dame', as she was known, and on learning that we were related to the Dame, they tugged their forelocks. That was an unexpected inversion of roles. They were unfailingly polite in their every address. One of them admired my winklepickers. That's what he'd wear, he said, given the freedom to choose. He showed me to his room. His pad was fantastically spartan with just a bed, a chair and a desk, and walls painted in hospital green. I fancy there was a little fire burning in a little fireplace, but my memory may have invented this. Though it was a world away, the facilities bore some resemblance to my erstwhile purple bedsit; it was like a scene from a BBC adaptation of

Dickens. I could hardly understand a thing my host was saying: his speech pattern made Billie sound like a pleb.

Back in Matron's pantry, the boys zoomed in for their afternoon tea, and zoomed back out again to zoom it down their necks. It was here that I witnessed at first-hand how the upper classes receive their taste in food, and their habits in eating it. It was Marmite on toast and bowls of cereal, and, as with the pace of everything else, it was no messing. They came back for second helpings, which also went down in a blur. Whenever I've dined with toffs it's always been the same; not only do they not give a fart about what's on the plate, they shovel it in as fast as humanly possible too, before any other boy can come along and steal it. It was like watching dogs clean their bowls.

I went back to Eton twice more. The next time we were invited down by the Dame to see the Christmas Revue, which was hosted by the broadcaster Richard Baker. Some years later I found myself working in the building trade in partnership with a public-school drop-out. He was another who had an untypical relationship with pop music; in his case his equilibrium was disturbed by it, it put him into a bad mood, so I was forced to listen to BBC Radio 4 all day long. I didn't mind, once I had become accustomed to it, because it improved my education, and I was keen on that. There was a certain amount of rubbish to put up with, though, including a programme called *Baker's Dozen* in which this Richard Baker pontificated on twelve pieces of light classical music in a show that would make Classic FM sponsored by Canon cameras look like highbrow broadcasting. Otherwise, Baker presented *Start the Week,* another irritating piece of radio designed to put you in a worse frame of mind than was necessary first thing on a Monday. *Start the Week* was a platform for Baker's mates to come along and puff their new books and plays.

I knew nothing about any of this, though, when I saw him compering the Eton Christmas Revue. I knew him like everyone else did, as a famous face from BBC television news.

The two most iniquitous points about this were: one, Eton had a Christmas Revue, which we did not have in Stoke on-Trent, and, two, they could pull in a big celebrity to MC it. The event was raucous, having all the elements one would expect from Cambridge Footlights (which I had read about in the *Guardian*): cross-dressing, comedy sketches, spoofs of teachers, and so on. The boys had a whale of a time, and afterwards there was drinking to follow. I could not compete with them at being posh, but I could compete with them at that. My tolerance was more than adequate, so I was able to watch them disintegrate into drunkeness while I remained a measure or two more sober.

Clive James, reviewing a biography of Kingsley Amis in the *TLS*, claimed that Amis, the 'suburban middle-class scholarship boy', though a natural Labour voter, was always wistfully responsive to the prospect of an 'elect tribe of upper-order males confidently at their ease'.

'He once told me,' James says, 'That he admired the way that they were *not bothered*.'

Being a working-class hero rather than a middle-class suburbanite, I wasn't bothered either. That was the tiny note of commonality between me and the 'Eton Rifles'. In years to come I would discover that there was enough spunk in me at least to tell the boss where he could stick his job: I was 'not bothered' enough to do that a few times until I became unemployable. That is one way of joining the ranks of the self-employed, which is a tangential method of changing certain perspectives.

The more pissed the Rifles got, the more I noted the occasional look of scorn. Our Dame was no longer there to protect us. What the hell were oiks like us doing in their boozer?

Hello hurrah, cheers then, mate!

Fuck 'em. I went outside to smoke a joint. I didn't know what I wanted to be, but I knew what I *didn't* want to be alright: I had no desire to be anything like that bunch of tools.

*****

I had given in my notice at the hotel. Liam and HRH the Rotund were dead set against my leaving for Europe with the Blond.

It's alright for him, they said, he's comes from a bit of money; but what are you going to do when you come back broke?

'I'll manage,' I said.

Liam and I had one final visit to Eton, out of term. It was then that I discovered the fact about the temperature of the water in the outdoor swimming pool. It was shaped like a bone – a long straight pool with circular diving pools at each end, with springboards, at either end. We weren't allowed into the water, officially; it costs thousands a term to buy the use of that facility. But Liam persuaded his mum to turn a blind eye. The sense of transgression only added to the frisson as we stood in our pants, poised to take the plunge. How many people from Stoke had ever done this?, I thought. None. I ought to have put my toe in first, but I didn't. The dive completely knocked the breath out of me; it must have been minus ten degrees: you had to swim like hell just to stay alive. I love the Stevie Smith poem, 'Not Waving But Drowning':

Nobody heard him, the dead man,
But still he lay moaning:
I was much further out than you thought
And not waving but drowning.

Poor chap, he always loved larking
And now he's dead

Something to Be

It must have been too cold for him his heart gave way,
They said.

Oh, no no no, it was too cold always
(Still the dead one lay moaning)
I was much too far out all my life
And not waving but drowning.

It works perfectly as a metaphor for all of those lives lived in quiet despair, but now, in this moment, it came to me that there was something more practical here, that there was a Guide to Survival, a guide that said: 'Foster, get the fuck out of that water and do it now!'

No wonder Eton was responsible for producing an army of heartless capitalist pigs and Tory bastards: simply participating in games was an exercise in survival-of-the-fittest. I both admired and was repelled by the conditions that I found here.

I had to try again. I had to be braver than this. I re-entered and found that by swimming as hard a front crawl as I could possibly manage, I could just about bear it.

Liam, who was faring no better than I was, found a way of saving the day by suddenly coming over wary of being caught. So we went to dry off.

The changing block was also outdoors: the spray that emerged from the showerheads was colder than the pool itself. This was the final straw. I had to concede it: I admitted a grudging respect for the scholars of Eton. You needed to be hard to go through this ritual, and no doubt the masters would make you do it in winter too, on days when you'd have to break the ice on the surface of the pool before you were thrown in for your mile and a half of compulsory butterfly. And no doubt they'd make you do it before dawn too. And no doubt they'd make you leave your pyjamas on as well, just to make it a bit more of a challenge. Small wonder they got through food like a pack of hyenas.

*****

Before we left for Europe, I dropped the Mini back up at Stoke where an acquaintance of Mother's would keep it safe for me in a lock-up. The Blond came along for the ride, and we had a night to kill. I knocked on the door of an old friend, looking to rouse a party of boys for a 'few bevvies', as the Blond always called a session. The friend was called Swifty.

Swifty came down to visit me in my very early days in London. He had rendezvoused in Soho with his cousin, who had come up from Southampton, so by the time I met them after my early shift was over they had arranged our evening's entertainment by purchasing three tickets to the Raymond Revue Bar. This was what many young men thought London was for: peep shows and live sex routines. There were only a very few people in the audience for this performance; our seats were in the front row (perhaps it was midweek). While, in theory, I could admire the bodies of the strippers, who seemed to have been chosen exclusively for their Junoesque physiques, in practice I could not, because I was too embarrassed by the whole thing, and, as part of my general political package, I was against the exploitation of women in this demeaning way too. But much more than that, I was disgusted by the soundtrack that was composed entirely of early seventies glamrock. At that point in time it was not possible to view early seventies glamrock through an ironic lens affording a veneer of retro-cool; it was only possible to hear it as utter crap.

Swifty had been working a nightshift. He came to the door in his slippers and his dressing gown. We had woken him. He didn't want to come out for a drink, but he wanted to be bought up to date, so I filled him in.

'What?' he said. 'You're giving up a good job like that? You must be mad.'

The Blond was appalled by my old friend's attitude. It was just about the worst thing he'd ever heard. As we walked away he said, 'It's only a hotel job. That Swifty guy was nineteen, man, he's gonna live in that house and do nightshift work all his life, isn't he?'

And then he laughed.

'What a hopeless case,' he said.

While I might have partially agreed with some part of that analysis, it was no place of his to discuss my people in these terms. It *wasn't* like London here; he ought to be able to see that. Jobs were everything. Jobs paid the rent, and paid off people like my mum, the credit drapery, the tally man, the loan shark, the debt collector, the stamps for the gas, the stamps for the electricity and the Christmas club. Mother was bemused by the turn of events in my career too. She liked the Blond, who put on a good show of being personable, but part of her shared the general view that the Europe scheme was hare-brained. Why had I studied two years at catering school if I was going to jack it in just to chase girls?

'And to see the world, Mum.'

'Oh yes, duck, and to see the world: why not fly to the moon while you're at it?'

'They don't seem too thrilled, mate,' the Blond said in a smug and irritating way as we stood blowing dope smoke out of the open window on the train back.

'So what.'

It was all I could reply. I didn't care for his tone. It was clear that he took the view that my people were somehow inferior to his, simply by being less metropolitan and less rich, when they had no choice in the matter on either count. What the hell was I doing hanging around with him? Still, the tickets were booked, and I'd worked my notice out. There was no turning back without losing face. And I was not going to be losing face, not in front of this bell-end.

The chambermaids went down to Athens three weeks ahead of us. I avoided Brigitte and the posh girl during this period and recruited a waitress to the temporary vacancy on the stud rota. The rock chick came to see us off, rolling up the almightiest five-skinner and making sure we smoked the whole thing before she'd allow us onto the Magic Bus. By the time we recovered from that we were in Switzerland with the munchies. At a service station we purchased the most expensive cartons of chips in history; they cost almost as much as the bus tickets. The journey took three days, most of which involved sitting in a traffic jam in Yugoslavia on the road to Zagreb. It was my first sight of a communist country; President Tito had died the previous year. The traffic jam brought out the worst in the residents of Yugoslavia: we saw men fighting each other for petrol at the roadside filling stations. It was not the best advertisement for socialism. But fortunately for me I was not provoked into a defence of left-wing philosophies because the Blond had no idea what the politics of the place were. To him, it was just the wild west. We changed a fiver at one of the filling stations, which bought us four peaches and two cans of Coke; we might have been naïve, but that didn't mean we didn't know we'd been ripped off. A fiver was a day's wages in Yugoslavia, it *had* to be worth more than that.

By the time we arrived in Athens we had everything that no human being desires: cramp, constipation, body odour, bad breath, greasy hair, zits, the lot. Even after the greatest shower of our lives in a communal block of the youth hostel in Athens, we were not looking our best. Moreover, upon rendezvousing with our trio of chambermaid babes, we discovered that they had been on the receiving end of non-stop hassle from Greek boys and Greek men for twenty-one days solid, and were entirely off the idea of sex. It was an inauspicious start to a couple of months that contained a more than usual amount of epiphanic moments.

It's unreasonable for me to go on about any of this at length, otherwise it will be like having to listen to an account of a Gap Year in Phuket. The salient points are as follows: I had a huge fight with the Blond, of course, over something I apparently said about Billie. I think I was suggesting that she had had an easier life than my own mother due to being richer. But we needed to fight anyway; we had to get a proper scrap going at some point, to indulge ourselves in the ritual necessity amongst young men of squaring up. We were no different from the drunks outside the Elephant in Fegg Hayes and we made the same declarations of love afterwards. We lazed about on the beaches of Greek islands with the girls for a few weeks, and then we took a ferry to Brindisi and hitch-hiked back up through Italy.

The Blond and I had a long-running argument about whose shorts were the more serious impediment to picking up lifts: my own were black with red, gold and green stripes down the seams, the international sign of Rasta. Whatever *he* said, it was undoubtedly his slightly-too-tight Union Jack boxers that were the greater handicap, and contributed most to a situation that saw us standing on motorway slip roads for hours on end, sipping on the dregs of warm Coke from near-empty plastic litre bottles.

We parted with the girls at some point near Pisa. It was sad, because they all had terrific bodies, great breasts and were often topless on beaches or in parks, and only scantily covered in the evenings. Quite apart from their general aesthetic beauty, their lovely breasts afforded us immense kudos amongst Italian boys, who would be happy to buy us rounds of drinks just as an excuse for staring at them for extended periods. Catholic girls, and Catholic codes (then, at least) were more coy. But our romantic relationships had come to nothing. The Blond was always arguing with his girl – not only were they at complete philosophical odds, she was also bulimic and a maniac. She had the greatest breasts of all, though; it was these that held their relationship together for as long as it lasted. Myself and the Southend thespian were playing out a charade of fancying each other. The truth was that our flame had burned only briefly before it died. I was much more interested in the third girl, the one who had been smart enough to remain unattached, who was the least conventionally good-looking, but who had by far the most stimulating mind, with which I had fallen secretly in love, of course. However much we might have potentially had in common – which I thought was quite a bit through the talk we'd had about poetry and politics and literature – she had me marked down as a philandering chancer and kept me at bay. The right decision. Even if our conversations were deeply promising, they did not eclipse the main event that my one-track mind was planning.

As autumn loomed into sight, the trio cashed in their Eurorail tickets and headed off to prepare for their studies back home. The Blond and I managed to get a lift from a truck driver right across to the bay of St Tropez. Here we sold ice creams and doughnuts on beaches on behalf of the local ice cream Mafia. We were paid *le peanuts* for our troubles, not even enough to keep us in bottles of gnat's piss beer from the hypermarché. We slept on the beach until one night we were robbed at knifepoint by Moroccan bandits. The following day we bumped into my mum, Henry and my sister Diane, who was all grown-up and fourteen now, on their annual holiday. We kept the robbery thing quiet, but all the same – 'Stephens, whattafuck are you a doin? You no hafta work at the ice creams when you gotta qualifications and a *certificates!*'

For once in my life I could see it from Henry's point of view: it didn't look too good. But I would hardly be doing it if I wasn't absolutely skint, would I? Still, I would not take money from them, principally because they did not offer any. You might find yourself fifteen hundred miles from home with your arse hanging out of your Rasta-striped shorts, but the rule of life is still the Stoke rule of life: let them learn the hard way.

I gave them some spiel that we had other work promised to us, grape-picking on a *vendange* (we had heard from the ice cream Mafia that this was soon to become available). In actual fact, we were so hard up that we had been forced into shoplifting, to eat. An experienced gang of Euro-bums had taught us the most efficient way to do it: take the tiny bit of change you've made from selling ice cream to the hypermarché and pick up baguettes and lemonade, a few francs' worth. Meanwhile slide sliced ham, sliced Emmental, duck paté, smoked trout – anything that comes in thin packs – down your pants under your shorts. Pick up individual pats of butter from the hypermarché café on the way out. Acquire melons and tomatoes from the fields. *Et voila: un picnic.*

In a stolen Mk III Cortina, owned by the experienced Euro bums – who were a charming gang of petty criminals whom we had met on the beach, originally from Watford – we toured the vineyards and sorted out two separate *vendanges*, one for the criminals, one for ourselves. The leader of the Watford Three was on the run. He had a blue Indian inkspot tattoo under his eye, a sign from prison, a signature that he'd already been inside. I thought being on the run meant that maybe he'd shot someone. But no, he was simply refusing to turn up in court to face a charge of shoplifting. 'What did you steal?' I asked.

'Duvets,' he said.

'Duvets? How in the name of blazes do you shoplift duvets?'

He mimed an act: one under each arm, and walk out all innocent-like.

'But why duvets, anyway?'

'Obvious, mate: easy to get rid of, innit: everybody wants a duvet – top tog rating, sweet as a nut.'

The Blond seemed to think I should know about this already, being northern and poor. It shouldn't be the case, surely, that southerners from Watford could trump me on knowledge of this type. I had spent my teenage years learning the kitchen French for cauliflower soup (Crème Dubarry, named after the *chouxfleur*-like hairstyle of Comtesse du Barry, mistress of Louis XV), and so on, not shoplifting blankets, but I could see his point.

Our *vendange* was at a run-down chateau owned by nice people who loaned us bicycles and gave us a cash advance so we could pay ourselves onto a campsite and get a shower. But, nice people or not, the work was back-breaking. It was a non-vintage vineyard in which the grapes trailed low to the ground. It was *le Vin du Plonk* they would be squeezing out of this lot, not *Nuits St George*. On our second day a Scottish boy with Midge Ure side-boards joined us, but he lasted only until lunchtime. He left with the line: 'I've had too much of a cushy middle-class upbringing fir this game.'

The Blond gained some esteem with me for being made of sterner stuff than that. In fact, had I only admitted it, it was I who would happily have followed Midge Ure out of the place. I hated grape-picking, I loathed its grim monotony, I loathed being coated in sticky juice all day long. And being the youngest, fittest-looking, and by far the most English labourers on site, we were given the hardest job, collecting up, in full-size plastic dustbins, the grapes from all the other slaves, slinging them onto our backs, and walking them over to a tractor. The driver of the tractor was a sadist who would always edge the vehicle just that bit further away each time we approached, so we had just that little bit further to walk in the ninety-five degrees of baking sunshine. The majority of the grape pickers were Portuguese peasants, whole families who had come up in caravans specifically for the seasonal harvest. This was *The Grapes of Wrath*, these were Steinbeck's Okies. I should have had fellow feeling for them, should have felt bonded by the International Code of Worker Unity, but I didn't. They appalled me with their gormless, toothless expressions, and their feral lunchtime fights for the last of the crumbs on the table. The Blond got on well with one of the younger girls, though, the throwback, the beauty. Judging by the wall-eyed glances he was getting from the male elders, I reckoned he was flirting dangerously, that he was looking to find a horse's head in his sleeping bag. The beautiful girl was impressed by his hair – there were no blonds in her world – and also by the signet ring that he used to wear, stamped with his family crest. I think she imagined he was from the nobility, fallen on hard times, and that one day he would arrive on his charger and take her away from all this, an idea that never crossed his mind.

Every night we ate steak *haché* and chips at the hypermarché and then we drank at the beach bars where the Watford Three stole beers and told us tales of the underworld. The beach bars played back-to-back Euro-hits and Euro-disco. I was fed up. I had had enough of being a tourist and a hobo. I felt like I was contributing nothing to the world and that I was wasting my life. Moreover, I had been deprived of culture for far too long. I had run out of books; by now I was reading the pulp fiction that holidaymakers had left behind, and I was so starved of stimulation I was almost enjoying it. I even read a Jeffrey Archer that the Blond had brought with him.

'GreatreadmateIseriouslyrecommendit.'

I lowered myself to reading the English tabloid press which, officially, I continued to boycott. I would have died for an incomprehensible sentence by Bernard Levin. When I came across a broadsheet it was a godsend, it could keep me going for days.

Euro-hits and Euro-disco aside, French taste in popular music was dreadful. They were fixated on the previous decade's MOR: if it wasn't 10cc trying to convince you that 'Life is a Minestrone', it was Supertramp whining on: *Take a look at my girlfriend, she's the only one I've got.*

The French seemed to be drawn to the dreck of English and American rock, and when you saw French punks they were just aping images they'd seen on postcards of the King's Road. There was no original attitude, there was no original detail, it was just copy-cat, blind latching-on to a style to which they added not a thing of their own. But how could you be a punk in the Med? What was there to complain about, what was there to rail against? Sunshine, paella, and beaches?

There were no mod revivalists either, though that would have at least made sense in the light of the principal form of youth transport – there were many, many scooters on the roads: one of the greatest sights I ever saw was a boy doing a wheelie on a Vespa through the steaming rush-hour traffic in the streets of Marseille. But there was absolutely *nothing* worth listening to in their indigenous music. The best that the pop 'stars' of Europe seemed to be capable of achieving was a pale emulation of Englishness. I began to feel hollow and starved of nourishment; I needed to know what was Number One on *Top of the Pops*. I needed access to a stove too: I needed to cook. I needed to restore my sense of self-worth. I came to understand that I was addicted to the routine of proper work – I had been doing it all my life, after all. I had my first paper round at eleven years old, and I had had a part-time job ever since, up until I began full time employment. The defining point about being working class to me, I began to understand, was the work, but the brain-dead activity of the *vendange* and the accompanying shanty town lifestyle had reached its end point. To get here I had seen the Acropolis, Pompeii, the Vatican, the Leaning Tower of Pisa, the filthiest toilet in the west, a Fiat 500 with 'Zoff' written on it in matt emulsion, the statue of David and Venice. I would always remember these, but what I had principally learned was that I could derive no pleasure from a life without job satisfaction.

The crop was in. The sadist edged away from us one last time in his wretched tractor; we caught up with the miserable bastard, threw our final loads into the back, and climbed in behind them.

'Peel me a grape, lad,' the Blond said.

The *vendange* provided us with enough francs to buy the bus tickets that would take us from the Promenade des Anglais in Nice all the way back to Victoria Station, SW1. We disembarked in similarly repulsive states of personal hygiene to those in which we had arrived in Athens three months earlier. London was cold and grey and miserable. It felt great. The Blond headed west to Fulham; I took the tube north to Euston, to catch a train to Stoke. It had been fractious between us over the last few weeks, but we could still call ourselves friends, just about. Back home I slept for two solid days and then I got back on the road, heading south once more in the single asset I had to my name, the black Mini with the white vinyl roof and the tinted-out windows.

By the end of the year my imaginary elder brother had released his last ever single and disbanded his group. I could no longer rely on The Jam to articulate and soundtrack my political views, I could no longer rely on Paul Weller for fashion advice. The era was changing. 'Pass the Dutchie', a reggae song about sharing a pipe by teenage novelty band Musical Youth, was Number One. This was succeeded in the top slot by 'Do You Really Want to Hurt Me?' by a group called Culture Club, who were fronted by a new breed of person called Boy George. Punk was dead, sexual ambiguity was *Top of the Pop*s: in 1982 the eighties finally opened.

*****

In the last couple of weeks before leaving for Europe I had rented the spare room at Billie's. I thought I might return to that base

camp, but it was a no go. Billie had had enough of the fathers
of waitresses calling in the middle of the night wanting to know
where their daughters were. A rule had been made that said that
it was time for Foster to take his dirty laundry elsewhere.

Excellent; I was homeless.

Immediately before stepping onto the Magic Bus I had
smoothed the way for Bumble to come down to London by setting him up in a temporary let with Brigitte Bardot (I lit the blue
touchpaper and ran like hell).

I found my brother changed on my return, in every way. His
ginger fop had been replaced by a blond mohican, his bondage
trousers by lycra shorts and plastic knee pads. He had found a
job in a cheap hotel in Bloomsbury, work to which he travelled
on rollerblades. In typical Bumble fashion, he became the first
known person to be cautioned for roller skating along the Edgware Road in a manner liable to cause an accident. If only he
could set that up as a routine event: it would be just like getting
the whip every day back at school.

Bumble had moved on from Brigitte (she had desisted from
taking him to her boudoir as an act of revenge on me, though I
heard that this was not down to any lack of effort on his part).
He'd rented a double bedsit in Willesden Green which he had
partially sublet to a pair of Siouxsie Sioux look-alikes. In the gruesome cider-soaked post-punk way of things, these two spent most
of their days lying in bed smoking cigarettes as if they were in an
art installation re-enacting the final hours of the Weimar Repub-
lic. Otherwise, the flat was vile, furnished with 1950s wardrobes
and matching wallpaper. The windows hadn't been cleaned for
twenty years; it was the sort of place that would give a purple
bedsit in Earls Court a good name. This residence was located
two streets away from Melrose Avenue, a road of no particular
note until I found I had to detour around it one day – the police
had cordoned it off due to the discovery of a batch of human

remains blocking the drains, a consequence of the activities of serial killer Dennis Nilsen, the civil servant who preyed on homeless, and often homosexual, young men and male prostitutes. That just about summed up Willesden Green. It was deathly squalid, even if it was a cultural melting pot. The principal accents you heard on the streets were Irish, Asian, Afro-Caribbean, drunken Scotsman and all varieties of the north (the Siouxsie Siouxs were from Speke). While none of these communities were famous for being well-heeled, lots of them were notorious for liking a fight. At night, in the area around the tube station, it was like being back home; one of the things I had liked about living in the central postcodes had been the absence of the post-adolescent male aggression that is so typical of northern street life, particularly at closing time. You always had to watch out for yourself when walking after dark in Stoke; there was usually a gang of Port Vale supporters swinging bicycle chains somewhere in the vicinity. I found the cosmopolitan attitude liberating and amazing; I had seldom seen a punch-up in Fulham or South Kensington or Notting Hill. But in Willesden Green, violence was always about to break out: Willesden Green was poverty-stricken, it had all the elements of lowlife and low-grade danger with which I was familiar from my early days back in SW5, but it had nothing in the way of the redeeming seedy glamour. Compared to life on Willesden High Road, the transsexuals and queens who had scared the shit out of me by flouncing up and down the platforms of Earl's Court tube station screeching away, being loud, proud and terrifying, were a tonic; the hordes of Pink Floyd fans who wiped out the entire contents of McDonalds and queued around the block all day spliffing up and lighting joss sticks seemed an exotic and beautiful memory.

But rental prices in Willesden were very cheap, there was that, at least. In the interests of establishing a little privacy and a roof over my head, I evicted the Siouxsies by locking them out until they gave up their Scouse whingeing ('Ya can't do dat: it's not fur!') and buggered off. I was penniless, had no job and had moved into a flat-share with Bumble. I had come back from Europe with nothing more than a tan. I was getting nowhere.

A return to the hotel world, maybe?

There were no superstar chefs in those days; in fact, the food that was served up in the hotels of the Savoy Group was distinctly mediocre, and the menus predictable. I considered presenting myself at the Dorchester where Anton Mosimann was building a reputation with his radical new technique, *cuisine minceur*: the method of cooking with no butter, no flour, and no cream that paved the way for the revolution that was *nouvelle cuisine*. *Nouvelle cuisine* was the biggest joke ever heard in Stoke: pay good money for two peas and an ablated prawn? You'd expect a mixed grill, a gallon of Bass and change for a taxi home for what you had to shell out on that. I liked the idea of *nouvelle cuisine*, the sheer nerve of it struck me as challenging, provocative and transgressive. But then I remembered the hours, the split shifts, the nights, and didn't apply anyway. My catering career was over.

I thought I'd see how the normal world lived, and got a job in an office instead. You could walk into a job centre and pick work up just like that. The office job was in the gas board HQ on Victoria Embankment, the kind of place where they serve biscuits on paper plates with cling film over them. It turned out that my job was to perform the role of Private Pike to Captain Mainwaring and Sergeant Wilson in Pipeline Planning. These two commuted in from the suburbs and spent most of their day talking about the relative merits and demerits of Toyota saloon cars. Pipeline Planning involved dealing with documents about pipes which might one day run under the North Sea, or, on the other hand, might not. As it turned out, I *had* picked up something else in Europe, besides the tan: itchy feet. The job was awful. I forced myself to stick it out for a fortnight in order to pick up the first pay cheque. Then I cleared my desk and left Capt. Mainwaring an explicatory resignation note which cited lyrics by Bob Dylan. Round the corner I got into my Mini, threw the parking ticket onto the pile on the back seat and hit the road for Southend, where my blonde ex-girl wasn't. I was looking for a easy lay, but I had forgotten: she had a life; she was studying to be an actress at college.

The following Monday morning I went to visit the rock chick. She had moved to Colindale to live with the seventies rocker. They were going to get married, which they did, one day. The groom wore a pink suit with the sleeves rolled up to the elbow. Some years down the line, when I was in the building trade, I invited my father to London to look after a job for me while my son was being born. We were at Billie's place – she acted as an agent in procuring work for me – and I caught the old man studying a framed photo of the wedding. London astonished him in many ways: the fat wedge that Cockney cowboys could pick up for botching plumbing work, the sang-froid that clients would exhibit in the face of my extraordinary quotations for decorating rooms, the price of bacon sarnies, the apparent absence of building regulations. But it was this wedding photograph that took the biscuit.

'What sort of person gets married in a pink suit *with the sleeves rolled up*, eh son?'

It was a rhetorical question.

The rock chick offered me a toke of her morning joint, as I knew she would. I was penniless – I could not even afford an eighth. The Monday morning spliff set me up for a tour of the job centres of north London. This time I was more specific: I was not cut out to be a company man, so I eliminated anything that involved office work. After a painstaking search – which involved an inevitable amount of corpsing at advertisements for jobs that required you to be fluent in Urdu for £2.75 an hour – I pulled myself together and came up with a possible. It was a position for which I had no qualifications whatsoever: work in shopfitting and exhibition stand erecting. I could wield a knife at a chopping board, that was one thing, but I was not practical in this way, I could not put a shelf up straight, or at all. The job also required a clean licence. There was driving involved, without it being an actual driving job. This I fancied, for the itchy feet. All the normal driving jobs required a specialist licence, an HGV or a PSV, and all the minicab work required that you own a 'four-door saloon'. I had neither the time nor inclination to acquire the specialist licences, I had not the funds to purchase a second-hand Mk IV Ford Cortina. I phoned the shop-fitting firm from a public telephone box which was full of ads for Harlesden tarts, who took a more direct approach than those in Earls Court: Miss Cummy, handjobs from a fiver, titwanks xxxtra.

The shopfitters offered me the job on the spot. I had turned up in a (two-tone Sta-prest) suit, and was given to believe that this slight effort of personal presentation, plus the gumption I'd demonstrated in undertaking the recent travelling in Europe, qualified me ahead of the other candidates.

It was a small family business. The HQ was at the foot of a ramshackle cul-de-sac in West Hampstead, where there was a small shanty town of lean-tos and corrugated sheds in which mechanics and panel beaters and welders lived. Our premises were the smartest of all these. There was a workshop on the ground floor, which was run single-handedly by the grandfather of the family, Frank. A rickety iron staircase took you to a drawing office upstairs, where the other family members made phone calls and drew up designs for exhibition stands and shop displays for firms that manufactured door furniture or fuses and electrical fittings. These businesses tended to be located on industrial estates somewhere in the middle of England where grants were given to stimulate the local economy, where land was cheap. Part of my work involved driving an antique Bedford van up and down the M1 or M40, ferrying display carousels back and forth between our HQ and theirs. The van had a sliding side door that would occasionally alarm me by flying open unannounced, and a gearbox that would occasionally alarm me by jumping out of gear at 75mph, the absolute top speed you could thrash out of it. These were small handicaps. I loved driving – it may have been mindless but it was at the same time scenic – and I was happy to be out and about, a free man. The company had one 'blue-riband' client, Polaroid. Polaroid had commissioned a batch of famous photographers to take pictures using a huge one-off camera that delivered prints at poster size. David Bailey was amongst them. One of my regular duties was to take these pictures to public buildings, to the library in Bradford or the theatre in Leicester, for instance, to hang the exhibition. This activity required a degree of aesthetic decision-making, and conferred upon me an atmosphere of artistic know-how, an idea that I did everything to encourage.

Otherwise, I was stuck in the workshop with Frank, whom I liked despite his never-ending supply of stories about the war. Frank was patient and taught me how to use workshop equipment and to become practical. This was a very handy, very transferable, free apprenticeship. We joined the design team upstairs for our lunches, where the conversation would often veer onto politics. Thatcherism was in full swing, worker discontent frequently featured on the news, industrial action was always taking place, and the miners' strike of '84 was around the corner. The members of the family firm were all big fans of Maggie; they only just about fell shy of having a framed picture of her on the wall. Thatcher was great news for them: being a grocer's daughter herself, she went out of her way to lower the elements of taxation that particularly affected small business – it was the 'crippling employment tax' her government had abolished that had made it possible to take me on, I was told. And, of course, the Tories would have nothing to do with a minimum wage; I was earning little more here than I was on flat pay at the hotel.

But the family helped me out by providing unlimited overtime at the same rate as the day work, and then Frank gave me a set of keys to the workshop, where I spent what was left of my evenings and weekends constructing plywood cabinets for the rock star and his assorted hangers-on and friends. In the blink of an eye I had become a freelance *designer*. There was no such thing as Health and Safety in small business; I had several more close dices with death – no person who has only just learned to operate a band`saw should be allowed to smoke a joint and then use it unsupervised when he is tired in the evening. Once again I was lucky; I never lost any digits, or any other body parts, though I did get bruised in the groin more than once from sheet material kicking back off the circular saw.

The workshop was an excellent facility for constructing these *hand-built, bespoke*, made-to-measure pieces of furniture. I drew up the *concepts* myself. The cabinets were commissioned to house state-of-the-art speakers, or the extensive collections of vinyl that belonged to my burgeoning client list. Some of these clients liked to make part-payment for the finished pieces with this new drug called cocaine. Like the grass they smoked, the 'Charlie' was exclusive, top-notch gear flown in direct from Bolivia, not the junk you'd get offered on the streets, or that people are palmed off with nowadays. This cocaine glittered like ice and made you feel invincible and offensively over-confident. You snorted it up your nose through a rolled-up bank note; the higher the denomination, the more flash and decadent you could feel. This snorting activity seemed to me to be dangerous. It was certainly not a natural thing to do, like smoking. But I had discovered through dope that no one dies, so I joined in. I loved it. In retrospect I am able to count my blessings that the £60 a gram it cost was well outside my tax bracket. That figure was more or less my basic wage, and a gram would allow for only one evening's pleasure for two (just about); the whole lot to yourself would be better. It was simple economics that prevented me from finishing up in the gutter, where one or two of the hangers-on found themselves. Unlike them, I had a small limit on my single credit card, so for me coke was for high days and holidays, but for some that I knew it turned into a five-hundred-quid a week habit when they were pulling in less than half that.

Still, I found myself looking into the gutter in any event, because one day I went home to find that the locks had been changed on the squalid bedsit. Apparently, we were months in arrears. I had been handing cash over to Bumble for the rent, but he had been using it for other purposes. This provoked one of the many rows that typified our time together. I was forced to call him several shades of a shit, though I was angrier with myself for being stupid enough to trust him to take care of the matter in the first place. I packed my bags into the Mini, which was more than adequate to contain all my worldly possessions, and went to live with a graphic designer from Melbourne in her flat in Cricklewood.

Sally was from upstairs at shopfitting HQ, and the only other non-family member on the payroll. She had been absent during my first weeks there, away back home in Australia attending a family funeral. She was as surprised to see me on her return to her drawing board, as I, in turn, was surprised to see her.

Sally was different from any girls I had previously had close association with. She was skinny, wore leather trousers and a mohair jumper, and had red hair in a feather-cut. Feather-cuts were not in at that point, but it looked very good. Melbourne, she advised me, was the only city in Australia that was not totally daggy.

'What the hell is daggy?' I said.

She just about refrained from saying that daggy was like me, a mod-revivalist Mini driver, a fan of mainstream bands like the Jam; a straight.

Sally was out of my league. She was a personal friend of Nick Cave and the Bad Seeds and loved the architectural motifs of the Bauhaus. The Pompidou Centre in Paris was her favourite building; books by Kafka and Woolf were idly strewn around her place. I had read about such lifestyles in the *NME*, but as an actual person, Sally was my first encounter with the avant-garde. Norman Mailer, who had been married six times, said that you never really get to find out about a woman until you meet her in court. I didn't intend getting as far as court, but I set about trying to meet Sally in the way I knew best. The pursuit involved settling into more than a few art cinemas to eat carrot cake and watch French movies directed by New Wave darling Eric Rohmer, films in which the actors improvised their lines while sitting under trees, or else gazing thoughtfully into the distance, while elsewhere nothing happened. There was always a sex scene in these movies and afterwards the woman would always wash herself using a bidet while simultaneously smoking a cigarette and berating the bloke about something he'd done, or hadn't done. I had to pretend this sort of thing was totally normal to me, watching a sex scene in the company of a woman you weren't going out with, but wanted to. It was quite an effort. I don't know that I liked the films, but I liked the *idea* of liking them. Apart from visits to the cinema, I would also meet Sally for those Sunday lunchtime Norwegian jazz sessions in pubs in Crouch End. Here we would meet her mates, who were the kind of people who are too cool to talk; they just posed, like extras in a Warhol movie. I really couldn't bear them, and after several months of fruitless hanging around I was ready to give up. Even though I had changed my wardrobe so that everything I wore was black, and even though I had accessorised this uniform with wraparound Ray-Bans which I kept on even in the dark, and even though I had switched from Camels to a rarer brand of cigarette called Prince, which came in a soft pack, and even though I permanently wore the one avant-garde item that I already owned, the Italian overcoat, there was still nothing doing. Sally's previous boyfriend had been stolen from her by the performance artist Laurie Anderson, of left-field pop fame: 'O Superman'. How could I compete with whoever *he* was? I continued to be mocked for my pronunciation, although by now I had severely modified the way I spoke. I could cite several influences on my new accent, influences including Essex bellboys, the Blond, Billie, HRH the Rotund and Paul Weller. I now talked in an awkward hybrid brand of southern Cockney posh with a Staffordshire bottom note. But though Sally had an Australian accent, like everyone else she would sometimes pause to ask me to repeat 'book' or 'bath', in order to be provided with a little light amusement.

Still, eventually, and finally, I discovered that the saying 'persistence can find its own reward' turns out to be true. I would go out of my way to help Sally, offering to make her cabinets from designer plywood, or to provide lifts in the Mini to anywhere she needed to be. One evening I made myself so useful as to commandeer the Bedford van to help her move flat, which involved several runs from Bethnal Green to Cricklewood and back. It was well into the small hours by the time we had finished. I ran over to my bedsit, from which I was imminently to be evicted, to pick up my stash, and we even shared a little Charlie too (not so daggy after all). Sally decided that it was time to take me to her bed, or rather her floor, where she dealt with me in a devastatingly effective and precise sexual manner that was highly avant-garde. There was no love involved. The sex was a triumph of form over content: mechanical and brilliant at the same time, it reminded me of a scene from this other *key text* film she'd taken me to see, Fritz Lang's *Metropolis*, a movie that was all about conveyor belts, technology, man as machine and de-humanisation. Later I was able to speculate that she had guided me to that movie as an insurance, in preparation for her bedtime manner.

I was seven or eight years younger than Sally. I was both an entertainment and a protégé, as well as a slight embarrassment: you can never be truly avant-garde if you are from Stoke-on-Trent. I retained some bad habits: I sometimes wore narrow leather ties, and I purchased a Pringle sweater, aping Weller, still, a bit, as he entered his Style Council phase. But eventually form followed content and we did fall in love. We spent every penny we had on culture, and partying, dancing through the night in the clubs of the warehouse scene, the forerunners of rave culture. The warehouse parties took place in abandoned locations in E1 or Brixton. There were drugs everywhere now: speed, acid, heroin, poppers, as well as the usual. I drew the line at anything you had to inject; I hated people who took heroin, they were debased, lying scum who would kill you for a fiver. I was a semi-detached member of this lifestyle; I lived it, but in the daytime I still worked with Frank and his stories of the Blitz, which I actually preferred: I wasn't a genuine player in the *demi-monde*. I wanted out. As I edged away, Sally became slightly clingy, so I fell out of love and moved on, like young men do, without having the decency to explain myself. I seemed to lack the emotional and psychological equipment necessary to even come up with a lame stereotypical tale explaining that I was too young to settle down or some old flannel like that. Instead, I elected to drop off the radar, a modus operandi that is possible in a city of ten million in a way that it isn't elsewhere. I quit the job, so I no longer saw Sally at work. The firm had started to treat me as one of the family to the extent that they had forgotten that this wasn't the case, expecting me to work eighteen hours a day during the peak exhibiting seasons for precisely nothing in the way of extra recompense, bar a couple of days off in lieu of the overtime payments I never got. Small business, I discovered, was a worse employer than a hotel. I had my nearest brush with death to date when, one night, having driven from London to Birmingham to drop off one trade stand, then on to Harrogate to single-handedly take another down, I was driving back to Birmingham (to be in place for an early start the next day at the NEC), when I fell asleep at the wheel. It was momentary, but my eyelids closed in the middle lane and reopened just as I was about to crash into the central reservation. That incident pushed me firmly into a course of direct action. In contrast to my inability to end things articulately with Sally, I found the appropriate form of Anglo Saxon words to tell the boss where he could stick his job. This resignation speech rendered me devoid of a reference, and effectively unemployable. To complete the runner, I also had to vacate Sally's flat, which I bravely did when she wasn't there.

*****

I had a new best friend by now and was spending all my free time with him in the pubs of Kentish Town, Camden Town, and South Hampstead, in those pockets where media types rub shoulders with drug dealers and drop-outs. The friend was one of the Blond's schoolmates; his name was Toby. Having a friend called Toby was on a par with having stripped floorboards and no carpets.

'He's got a friend called *Toby*.'

There are no Tobys in Stoke, and there never were. First names tended to be lifted from a partial reading of the New Testament – Mark or John, yes; Matthew or Luke, no. Otherwise, they were functional: Robert, Trevor, Steven. Steven with a v was the original spelling of my own name. It was when I had my first business cards printed, for my own decorating company (which I called

'A Bigger Splash', the name of a rock band that I used to see advertised on fly-posters – I had never heard of the painting by Hockney) that I changed it to a ph. I thought this would help; I thought v was for a footballer, whereas ph was more appropriate for a sophisticated, creative *designer* such as myself.

Toby's parents owned a house at the foot of Hampstead Heath. Michael Palin lived round one corner, Michel Foot round the next. I had seen Foot before; he had a friend that he used to visit at Claridge's Hotel. The friend was a silver-haired bastard, and a Sir. He was one of an elite number of guests who were in permanent residence there (imagine the cost of that), persons who lived in circumstances in which they were waited on hand and foot every day of their lives. The American actress Elaine Stritch was another full-timer, for a while. She was often to be found wearing a leopard-skin print dressing gown in a waiter's pantry, a fag dangling from her lips, making herself a slice of toast. She was held in affection for her self-catering eccentricity as well as for her smoking, which was epic: not only between courses, but also during them. The Sir was not held in any affection at all. He was rude – which is always counter-productive when it comes to waiters, only ensuring that they spit into your coffee pot – and had a mad Hungarian wife, an exceptionally bad-tempered and antique flyweight ex-ballerina. She had two moods: furious or furious and self-pityingly tearful. She would occasionally cling to your arm saying that 'Soon Sir would die... and then whatever would become of *her?*'

Foot's treacherous friendship with this couple did not go unnoted, though neither did it stop me from my automatic default Labour vote (it was the dreary, trammelled, politically correct, dogmatic cant of *New* Labour that did that). It gave me a privileged insight into what actually goes on behind the scenes. I thought it contemptible that a prominent party figure, and *future leader*, should find time to fraternise with Sir and the ballerina, when he was apparently on our side.

Toby and I rented a flat at the top of a house in Kentish Town. It was my most spacious let to date, having *two* rooms as well as a kitchenette and shower cubicle. It was furnished in the usual sordid manner, but with my newly acquired DIY skills I could improve that. This would be my first effort at gentrifying my living space; I built an open-plan wardrobe for the important matter of storing and displaying our clothes.

Toby's mother lived half a mile away in Gospel Oak, in a four-storey Victorian terrace with a front door with stained-glass panels. The ground floor of this property consisted of a separate flat, which she sublet. This meant that their family living room was on the first floor, an interior arrangement I'd never encountered before; to look out of the front room *down* onto the street outside struck me as rather chic. The room itself was large, with several big sofas sculpted into comfortable shapes by years of extensive use. There were corduroy scatter cushions and bean bags; there was a wide, low coffee table spread with back issues of the *Observer* magazine, the *New Statesman*, the *Economist*, and *Private Eye*; there was a guitar, there were ethnic rugs, and, of course, there were stripped floorboards. Penguin classics and poetry lined the bookshelves. In the bathroom a framed film poster for Ruth Prawer Jhabvala's *Heat and Dust* hung on the wall. Toby's mother looked like Carole King on the cover shot of the *Tapestry* album. She was less the sort of older woman you would jerk off about than the kind you would entertain fantasies of marrying. This was an idea that was in the realm of the possible, because, of course, she was separated from Toby's father, a businessman who kept a flat in Hampstead, and properties elsewhere. He was called Hugh and he would occasionally take us out for four quick pints of bitter and some cynical words of wisdom in an olde world pub in nearby Highgate, a district that was so tree-lined and beautiful that it seemed to be a village in the country. Even though some of

Hugh's words of wisdom consisted of an attack on left-wing politics, I liked him. He was affable and charming, a sharkish version of Richard Briers in *The Good Life*. The other drinkers in the olde pub were an assortment of drunks, queenly actors fallen on hard times, plus more English businessmen in the off-duty uniform of cable-knit jumpers, Barbour jackets, wide-wale corduroy trousers with turn-ups, and brogues.

We were out of place in there, but only just. I remained loyal to the Italian overcoat. Toby wore his hair in a sub-Joe Strummer DA haircut and his wardrobe was selected from a limited palette of classics – Levi 501s, Doctor Martens, decent shirts and a second-hand overcoat from Camden Market. He was cool, and he was a maniac. He worked in a film office in Soho, engaged in duties that seemed to consist almost entirely of running around having a good time. We would meet after work every day to begin drinking and smoking, which was what we did seven nights a week. And then we would move on to a night club. We constructed our dual identity through our prodigious intake of whatever we could get our hands on: if we were aiming to emulate anybody, it must have been Keith Richards. We converted to vegetarianism for a while, as not eating meat was the only healthy thing we could think of doing: a small consolation to our bodies, an apology for the way we treated them the rest of the time. Our version of vegetarianism consisted of having sausage, egg, bacon, chips and beans without the bacon or the sausage.

Toby's mother took an interest of sorts in me, though not of the wedding bells variety that I may have had in mind. She identified me as a case that would benefit from the nourishment of further education. She was studying for a degree in English at one of London's universities; she was the first mature student I had ever encountered. For my birthday, she gave me three books: *The Third Policeman* by Flann O'Brien, *Turtle Diary* by Russell Hoban and *The Image Men* by J.B. Priestley. The O'Brien was the literary classic; the other two, though more middle-brow, were not the sorts of novel I would have picked up if left to my own devices. *The Image Men* was a satire about two down at heel academics who shake themselves up and achieve mid-life success by setting up a PR company, rebranding themselves in the process of rebranding other items. The central theme of this novel, first published in 1968, was about to become bang up to date: the eighties were kicking in properly now; the decade of consumerism was gearing up.

When Gordon Gekko in *Wall Street* said that Greed was Good, the movie was simply holding up a mirror to the new world order, a world order that suited the Blond, who had found employment in some commercial print operation, and who was increasingly surrounded by the young coiners who were commissioning the commercial print, many of whom worked in advertising. These were company men; making money was their *raison d'être*. The *raison d'être* had one principal purpose: to enable one to get a foot on the property ladder. Any cash that remained after meeting the monthly mortgage payment could be invested in filling the property with designer accessories, buying drugs and purchasing cars. The Golf Gti was the model that would announce that you were on the up, the Porsche 911 that you had arrived.

Mineral water arrived onto the supermarket shelves of London from France. Nothing could have made my auntie Mary's face turn sourer than the sight of a bottle of Perrier: the bloody stuff comes out of the tap for free: *they've more money than sense down there.*

Suddenly there was nothing that could not be embellished with the description 'designer'. If you couldn't be bothered to shave you could copy George Michael and call your growth designer stubble. Those with access to a fat wad, and the credit rating that came with it, could listen to the new compact disc by

Wham! on a minimalist hi-fi designer system made in Denmark by designer darlings Bang & Olufsen while drinking a bottle of designer Mexican beer out of a designer Mexican bottle with a designer wedge of designer lime shoved in the designer top. In this way the effete, girly drink of 'a half of lager and lime please' became a desirable designer tipple and cost more than a proper pint of macho bitter.

Wham! were at the frontier of the new breed of good-time synthesiser pap. The situation had returned to normal in the wonderful world of Radio 1. Political posturing, which had never had any rightful place in pop, had been more or less eradicated. Chart music reverted to its usual default position: boy meets girl, boy loses girl, time can never mend the careless whispers of a good friend that let you down bad. Punk was dead. The new groups wrote songs in which the personal took precedence over the political, doodling out lyrics that were more likely to consider the correct temperature at which to serve a piña colada than they were the Cold War. The new breed of pop musician did not renounce the struggles and ethics of punk so much as they did not care about them in the first place; that was then, and this was now. Preoccupations were different. Birmingham's Duran Duran and their Islington counterparts in Spandau Ballet were more concerned with dressing up nice and dandy and choosing the right shade of lip liner than they were with the people's right to work. Where punk had been essentially dour, this new order was a deregulated land of cash and fun. I was against fun in music; to me it was a misappropriation of the only art form that young people could commandeer to bring about change. Some of the new music, superficial though it was, sounded great; you couldn't say it didn't, but what was the point of that?

The point of that was obvious: all the time and effort that was spent on production generated an ever-increasing need for better hi-fi systems on which to keep up with the quality of the sound.

The point was to stimulate consumer purchasing. Freedom of choice was the buzz expression. Freedom of choice implied only one thing, which was not the freedom to take books out of the library, but the freedom to spend money. In practice – to generate this money – London saw the emergence of a new strain of stressed-out twenty-somethings working eighteen-hour days. These individuals unwound in cocktail bars. Wearing T-shirts emblazoned with the legend 'Frankie says RELAX', the upwardly mobile striver did just that by downing champagne as if it were lager, tooting coke as if it were speed, and tearing up to Norfolk at the weekend for a spot of country cottaging. Monday to Friday was spent coining in as much as possible by privatising everything in sight. Yuppies were everywhere. Driven by the creed of conspicuous consumption, they were obsessed with self-image – if you were not rich and successful, you were nobody. This was a cult in which surface took over from substance; one transaction that could never take place with a yuppie was an intelligent conversation.

Under the surface, in a different world, other non-designer, non-consumerist events were gathering momentum. The miners' strike of '84 arrived in Camden Town. Northern lads with mad, faraway looks in their eyes stood outside the bong stalls rattling buckets for change; later you would find them in the public houses expressing disbelief about the price of ale, eating hash, and trying out the usual pissed-up grope routines. I bumped into an ex-miner who I knew slightly from the Elephant, a man called Dekka. Dekka was handsome and particularly tough-looking, his face was marked with the blue scars that some miners pick up when coal dust gets into cuts and the skin grows over it, a form of tattooing. Dekka's approach to romance was a succinct variation on the drunken grope. In his inside pocket he carried a Polaroid picture of his erect member. He used to pull this out and show it to the ladies as a kind of calling card. How successful this was in

Stoke, I don't know, but it was an absolute non-starter in north London: even the frivolous party-type girl who loved Andrew Ridgeley out of Wham! tended to recoil at Dekka's antediluvian version of a chat-up line.

Dekka had retired from mining on some sort of disability pension and he was down in the Smoke for the jolly, for a few days out. He was on a virtual holiday. I echoed his spirit on those several occasions when I accompanied the miners on their rallies through London. There were often free gigs at the end of these marches where the Redskins and Billie Bragg, or Gil Scott-Heron and other radical dudes from Washington DC performed on stages set up on Clapham Common or in Hyde Park. These events were open-air clubs with excellent potential for picking up girls; they were epicentres insofar as sourcing feminists went: *Spare Rib*, the Socialist Workers Party, the Communist Party of Great Britain – all went along for the ride. If pretending to be a vegetarian only got me halfway, I might have to take the matter further by reverting to my original accent. I latched up with Lottie, the girl with the No Truck with the Chilean Junta! poster, through exactly these means. I was intrigued with Lottie's thinking, even though it seemed to me that her beliefs and thought systems were often confused. We sat in a vegetarian restaurant in Holloway Road one evening while the man at the next table described to his female companion how much better he felt now that he had 'learned to cry'. I listened in disgusted embarrassment as he went on about his new ability at blarting (as it's known in Stoke). It was just about the worst thing I'd ever overheard; it was a real low for me to sit dipping pitta bread into vegetable stew while he droned on about his newfound talent. I'd have jumped for joy to have seen one of my Cockney bellboys run past wafting his wad at me, or for Dekka to turn up and flash his Polaroid. Outside I voiced my thoughts, which I'd kept to myself at the table of 'The Earth Exchange'. Lottie ticked me off for being such a macho dinosaur, although it was my bona fide credentials as a working-class, non-blarting, hero that had interested her in the first place. Which I mentioned too. There was more contradictory behaviour when I found myself having to wait in a pub while she visited her girlfriends in a café round the corner, a café that was a 'man-free space'. Keen student that I was of alternative culture, I didn't know that anything as sinister as this was going on. Lottie was against the persecution of people on the grounds of race or gender, of course, though men seemed to constitute an exception to this rule. I mentioned this too. I argued the point, so she repeated her stuff about the generations of oppression wrought by patriarchal society as represented by the likes of me, to which I replied that she could sort her own fucking orgasms out in future then, since I was such a swine. That was fine by her; we called it a day.

I was gentleman enough to sarcastically offer her a lift home, free of charge, in the minicab I was driving. This was what I had resorted to doing for work. Following the incident where I had advised the exhibition boss to go swivel, I bought a bench vice and a few other tools and set up a business in our flat. The first item I constructed under these conditions turned out to be a rhomboid record cabinet, which I might have got away with six months later, perhaps passing it off as a radical new design. But neither I, nor my clients, were quite that advanced yet, and this one was supposed to be rectangular. Trying to run a workshop without the aid of power tools, from a kitchenette, was hopeless. I could have signed on, but I had always resisted the dole office. I had taken a look inside once or twice, both back home and here, and had found that I could not get myself to cross the threshold into the waiting room where the stench of resignation reeked as heavily as the cloud of cigarette smoke. The dole office was the antechamber to despair. I would not let the absence of money force me in there. I had a certificates and a qualifications; I was better than that.

My attitude to state benefit, combined with my lack of a reference, left me looking at the smallest of small ads in the jobs column of the *Evening Standard*. Here I found a possible. There was one minicab company out of all the many minicab companies that advertised the requirement for 'own four door saloon' that instead said 'vehicle provided'. I phoned, from a red phone box.

'When can you start?' the man at the other end said. 'Can you do today?'

I began on the nightshift. There was no training, the base was in West Hendon, a place I had never been to, though it was only three miles north of Kentish Town. I had to consult the A-Z just to get there. The vehicle provided was, as I anticipated, a Mk IV Ford Cortina. It was on the road 24/7: the day driver – an Indian called the Professor – got out, I got in. There would always be some small matter amiss with this Cortina, a bald tyre or two, the absence of an MOT, a lapsed insurance certificate, something like that.

One weekend when the car was actually off the road (the big end must have seized), I drove home in my Mini. I pulled into Watford Gap services, where the Metropolitan Police (who were being sent up as reinforcements to help out the constabularies of Nottinghamshire and South Yorkshire) were changing shifts. There were at least thirty busloads on either side of the carriageway. They were everywhere. A group of Asian youths walked past them, deliberately spliffing up. Not a single cop took the slightest interest, which surprised me. I hung around with a coffee and a cigarette and studied them closely, while they drank their own coffees and smoked their own cigarettes. There was little conversation amongst the men, and less banter. They were in the zone, focused on something. They were preparing for war.

History records who won and who lost, though I could never

see the inevitability of the outcome until after it had happened. Towards the end there was an enormous march, a final push. It took place on a Sunday, beginning in the morning and culminating in an afternoon rally in Trafalgar Square. I took Toby down there for a day out. We did not march; instead, we got to the square early and climbed into the bowl of one of the fountains (it was switched off), a vantage point that gave the best available perspective on events. From our elevated position we looked straight down Whitehall, from where the marchers filtered into the square behind their colliery banners for the closing speeches by Ken Livingstone and Tony Benn. We were the first two persons on that fountain, but it soon filled to the edges, mainly with miners from Sheffield. Young men from Stoke and Sheffield might be expected to approach each other in a suspicious and hostile manner on the basis of local and regional in-fighting founded on football rivalry and accent-dislike: Lancashire hates Yorkshire, Staffordshire reviles the Black Country, and so on. But these were not normal circumstances. Everybody in the north was allied now in a specific hatred of two groups: the strikebreakers from the Nottinghamshire coalfield (twenty years later supporters would still sing 'scab' to Nottingham Forest fans at football matches), and the other traditional hatred, of the south as represented by the Tory government and, now, more concretely, by the police. Coming from Stoke and Sheffield under conditions such as these was to stand shoulder to shoulder on the fountainhead. I noted, though, that Toby was looking uncomfortable and that he kept quiet. He didn't want to announce his southern provenance, and I didn't blame him: our companions were pumped up, full of barely suppressed aggression, and they were becoming increasingly agitated; from the outset I had reverted my own accent back to its default sound, or as near as I could get it.

Our platform was becoming dangerously overcrowded now. Just as I was beginning to feel fraudulent for our taking up two of the spaces that rightly belonged to actual mine workers, the Sheffield posse deserted their post: they had spotted an opportunity, one that had been a long time coming.

The square was jam-packed, beyond capacity, though the marchers continued to pour in, stretching back as far as the eye could see. This situation forced a line of police with riot shields, backed up by a second line on horseback, to cut the marchers off some way into Whitehall. It looked a provocative decision, and, of course, the marchers jumped to the conclusion that once more they were being made the victims of oppression and were having their civil liberties removed. From my viewpoint I could clearly see the rationale: it was a crowd control issue, the police simply had to make an effort to prevent a crush in the square. Whitehall is a very wide thoroughfare, the blocked-off marchers numbered thousands and they began to make use of whatever they could lay their hands on as missiles to hurl against the police lines. The opportunity that the Sheffield boys had identified was twofold: firstly, this was the first time for months that *they* had outnumbered the coppers – they had been talking about it excitedly for most of the time they were with us. Secondly, someone from Westminster City Council had dropped an almighty bollock: behind the police lines a flat-back truck stacked with temporary crush barriers had been left parked on a pavement. I kept sight of my gang as they made their way down to this truck. They hoisted themselves up onto it and began pelting the police with these barriers, which were large, heavy, flew through the air like frisbies and constituted genuinely offensive weapons. It took only seconds for more to join in. There was an avalanche of metal flying into the coppers, the horses, and bystanders too. It was carnage; it was the single most violent civil event I had ever seen, which was saying something: I had grown up with seventies football hooliganism, with running gangs, and mobs round every corner. Knuckledusters and knives were put into use at Stoke City matches all through my teenage years. Stoke fans had a reputation as superb fighters and other clubs saw that as a challenge; some of those who fancied it brought big crews along to our place. Against certain teams – Wolves, Burnley, Spurs – the football took second billing to the main event: tribal warfare. I had witnessed it often enough to be able to announce a verdict on what I saw in front of me now: though both sides took casualties, for once, the miners could claim a victory.

I had insisted we stay to watch, though Toby had long since had enough. These were not his people, this was not his scene. Finally, we slipped from the fountain and headed back towards Kentish Town. We talked about it on the way as we walked up past the theatres and cinemas of Shaftesbury Avenue, where Toby might rather have been spending his time. Toby's grandmother had put some money into a production of Joe Orton's *Loot* at one of these theatres. We had been given complimentary tickets to a preview night, where we sat next to the actor couple John Alderton and Pauline Collins. I quite liked it – I thought it was my kind of thing, even though the play was a farce, even though it was being staged at a theatre: I made an effort to like it because I knew that Orton was a working-class hero like me, and from the Midlands too, even if it was only Leicester. He was a local boy made good.

I was energised and pumped up as we walked on now; a primitive part of me, the part that had run (away) at football matches thought the battle had been great. I had witnessed that sinister shift change on the M1, the foot soldiers of the Met being sent up to suppress my people, and I was delighted to see them getting what they deserved. In my view, lining up with riot shields hundreds of miles away from their own manor was a duty that the policemen should have refused to carry out. They had their own federation; they could have held a ballot and decided to act against it, couldn't they? They might have precipitated a general strike if they'd seen fit, and brought the government down on behalf of their fellow workers in the process. I saw that as a real possibility. But of course, the Met were southerners, on tasty mass-suppressing overtime bonuses; they were Cockney-Essex bellboys promoted into fascist uniforms. They were agents of the state. They were lowlife.

Later that day I went out of my way to ensure that I caught all of the evening news bulletins on television, wondering, vainly, whether I might spot myself on top of the fountain, or catch sight of my brothers-in-arms from Yorkshire engaging in their heroic act of guerilla war. It was still Sunday, so the bulletins were shorter than usual, but perhaps there would be a special extended news, with all this going on.

There was nothing, not a single, solitary mention. I have never known it before or since, but it was a news blackout. The Tory boot boy Norman Tebbit used to devote hours of his airtime to claims that the BBC was full of lefty sympathisers, biased against the Conservatives; he never missed an opportunity to make a veiled threat about abolishing the licence fee. He'd certainly bought them off here, and he'd got ITV and Channel 4 in on it too (that was your lot – it was pre-satellite, and pre-cable.) I pictured all the correspondents taking a well-earned rest, browsing through holiday brochures and sipping Pimms on their patios and roof gardens. I drank a Mexican beer with a sliver of lime stuck in the top of the bottle. You had to hand it to Thatcher, she'd got them on the run, she'd got them tucked up good and proper in her stiff, starched apron pocket. I don't know how she'd done it, but she'd put the frighteners out.

With the news editors fallen into line, the writing was on the wall. It was only a matter of weeks before the strike was called off. It had lasted nearly twelve months. In the end they starved the men back to work.

A year or so later I was working on a building site, looking after a gang of boys from Glasgow, complete chancers (not unlike me) who came to work kitted out in Celtic shirts and bobble hats. One of them, Marko, had equipped himself with his tools by creeping along the roofs of Earls Court, from the flat in which they were holed up, and stealing them from the scaffolding of a nearby house that was being renovated. He was about to begin tarring a roof on our site when he said, 'Steve, do you get seagulls in London?'

'No,' I said.

There was a very long pause.

'No. Are you sure?'

'Yes, I'm sure. Why?'

'You can tell what the weather's going to be like from the seagulls – I want to be certain it's worth starting: rain will ruin the job.'

The seagulls were a delaying tactic. Judging by the mess he made when he did finally start, this had to be the first time in his life that Marko had tarred a roof: rain would have made little difference one way or the other.

Marko smoked and drank more than anyone I've ever met, with the exception of his friend Lenny. Lenny was what they called 'a pure bear', a rugby player who had worked down the pit. Lenny had marched back to work alongside his uncle and his dad, the brass band playing, and all the old men 'greetin', the Scottish word for blarting.

'That was it for me,' he said. 'No way could I take ma sen back down there wi grown men greetin, greetin like babies.'

And so, instead, he and his mates had decided to head south to where the streets were paved with gold. They moved on from that one room that they all (they were five in number) shared in Earls Court to a two-room flat in Tooting Bec. It was one of this five, the outcast, the Hun (the Rangers fan) who I saw, with my own eyes, performing 'Hey Big Spender' on the last tube home. When I critiqued his performance a couple of days later, a couple of days before he headed back home, he remembered nothing about it; their drinking was epic. The rest of the gang arrived at work on a Monday morning with their hands trembling and without a penny left from Friday's pay packet. The only reason they came in was to get a sub to keep them going until they signed on on a Tuesday. They could never understand why I didn't do the same.

I had certainly been skint enough to justify it in those weeks when I was trying to run a joinery from the kitchenette. The tooling-up, plus the purchase of materials – not just the timber, but the glues, the pins, the tacks, the screws – all those sundries that I had picked up for free when I was doing foreigners out of Frank's workshop – meant that I was spending more to produce the goods than I was able to overcharge, even to those coke fiends who worked in the music business. The loose change that I tossed into miners' buckets came out of my unauthorised overdraft: one high street bank closed a current account on me; the next I tried soon followed suit.

My need for funds had become urgent, this was where the minicabbing came in: here was an activity that would at least put hard cash directly into my empty pockets.

But in my first weeks on the circuit I continued to be a financial black hole. The deal was that *you* paid *them* a fee of £100 a week, for the car and for the jobs they supplied. Then you put the petrol in the tank. Then you paid for your own crash repairs (what with the difficulty over the insurance documents); anything that remained after that was yours. In my first days this made me as flush as a Glaswegian at the beginning of the week.

I was given a call sign: Zero Three. The caller, Woody, gave the jobs out over the air. I would receive a message: Zero Three, go to Glitterhowse, mate.

Woody was the most authentic Cockney in the whole of history. His instruction came through the ether, punctuated by pockets of static, as follows: Zerofreegataclirarrsmay.

Having asked him to repeat the instruction six or seven times (and discerning no variation whatsoever in his pronunciation), Woody would eventually give up on me in exasperation and pass the job on to Zero Four. I would hear him acknowledge Zero Four's PoB (Passenger on Board) about ten minutes later and I would curse and smack the steering wheel in frustration.

But even if I had understood him, I would have had very little hope of discovering that Glitterhowse was 'offovvnorfcircular' and that however desperately I had been flicking through the G index of my A-Z to find out where the hell 'gataclirarrs' might be, it would not have been marked in any event because it was not a street, was spelled with a C, and in fact was a block of flats, and situated offova road beginning with B, called Brent Way.

There is a dead spot on the nightshift between 3.30am and 5am, before the morning jobs start to come in, jobs where you drive other shift workers from East Finchley to Golders Green for their early starts at underground stations, where the grilles are still up from the night before. I used the dead time to study the A-Z and to drive around, almost alone, unfettered by other traffic. In this way I conducted my own reduced version of the Knowledge, the test that proper licensed black-cab drivers have to complete before they are allowed to start working (black-cab drivers always cut up minicabs: it's the least they can do to gain the smallest retribution on that fly group of individuals who simply step into a four-door saloon and get straight to work without spending four years on a moped with a clipboard). Seeing the roads empty like that afforded me a whole new sense of the topography of the capital: I suddenly saw it as a rather beautiful place, and I began to feel that by knowing its geography intimately, I actually belonged there. In addition to generating these abstract feelings, my perambulations enabled me to become a semi-competent minicab driver. Which, in context, is a competent mini cab driver. I could not live with the idea of myself being the sort of clown who does not have the first notion of which direction the West End lies; I had some sense of professional pride even if I was sharing a Mk IV Cortina with a sham professor. The Prof was a Prof of Love. Once he had decided he had nothing in particular against me, he would bring gifts of samosas and lime pickle into the car for us to share, gifts for which he would charge me the full amount, including enough to cover *his* portion, all the while describing the splendid ways in which he would like to make passionate love to certain of the passing girls. He had crazy eyes, a full beard, and wore a collection of exceptionally unkempt brown shirts. He would sometimes make sexy faces at the passing girls through the car window.

'Don't do that, Prof,' I'd say. 'Look, you're frightening them.'

'Nonsense, stupid boy,' he would reply, tapping his nose, as if to assure me that his approach was not only tried and tested, but that moreover it was foolproof, that it was bound to persuade one of the lovely ladies to stop short saying, 'O, Prof, please come round to my boudoir *this instant* for a mind-blowing session of tantric sex and bring your friend and your lime pickle and your snacks with you while you're at it: I have a lovely twin sister back home, she is always hungry for a chapatti and well up for a foursome.'

As with all the other minicab drivers, the Prof was a man who had something missing from his life; in his case it was quite simple – he never had a girlfriend.

The very least that the remainder of my fellow drivers did not possess was their own four-door saloon. Most of them were a decade older than me, at least. I was in the company of desperados. Mike was an alcoholic from Blackburn who regularly challenged people to drinking races in the local pub, races he never lost. One day a faulty brake light saw Mike become the object of a police chase along the Hendon Way, and while he was PoB, too: very, very bad form, even amongst cowboys like us. When the cops finally boxed him off, Mike ejected and ran for over half a mile until he was floored somewhere near Staples Corner. How he got that far with the six or more pints he had inside him was anyone's guess. He was never seen again. Another short-lived employee of Relay Cars had changed his name to Sonny, a decision that provoked a considerable amount of speculation regarding the heinous nature of his real name. Sonny wore a full-length leather overcoat at all times. This cab driving was just temporary work for him; his professional career took place in the summertime on the Costa del Sol, where he ran a holiday resort that he also owned. Sure he did. Then there was Alfie, an endless tipster of horses that never, ever came in. Liars, dreamers, mad dogs and chancers, one and all.

Where did this leave me?

Everyone had something to say about this line of work. Toby was against it because of the stupid hours, which worked against spending every night in the pub before moving on to a night-club. Though I *did* come in very handy for picking up members of our circle, post-nightclub, this completely missed the point of being in a circle in the first place.

The Blond thought it was work for dregs, the road to nowhere; back in Stoke my mum gave of her best. 'If it makes you happy…'

Henry treated me to his exasperated line: 'Why you wanna be a taxi driver for a Stephens when you got a qualifications and a *certificates*?'

The Blond was right, it was the road to nowhere. But equally, there was something in it for me: there was a feeling that I had never quite known before, a complete freedom from authority: though there was a boss, he took the expression laissez-faire to an extreme – you had to do something criminal in order to be sacked. Laissez-faire was an expression that I had learned in the economics lessons that we'd had at catering college. Laissez-faire was the central tenet of Tory politics: let the market rule. What I considered abhorrent as a political creed, I found suited me very well in personal terms. After a few months, I had graduated up the ranks and I was rewarded with my own Mk IV Cortina; I no longer had to share. In this way I could be driving around in my free time listening in to what was happening and just drop in to pick up some cash if there were good jobs going begging when driver numbers were low. Likewise, I might fall off the radar if the distractions on offer were worth it.

On top of my own free-market decisions, there was also the chance to experiment with several new personas. I could be very Cockney, or very northern, depending. I could be slightly posh, or slightly rough, depending. On the dashboard I kept a copy of *Prick up Your Ears*, the biography of Joe Orton. I picked it up after seeing the production of *Loot* that Toby's grandma part-financed and I read the book during quiet moments. I kept a spoon in the car – I would buy a yoghurt from a petrol station and park up in a cul-de-sac under a street light. Orton's life fascinated me. He lived his days in similarly shabby circumstances to those in which I currently found myself. He ended those days by getting himself killed by his lover Kenneth Halliwell, in a rented flat in Noel Road, Islington N1. When gentrification was kicking in with a vengeance, I worked on restoring a four-storey Georgian terrace two doors along from that very house. It was my first job in the building trade, a career move that came about as a consequence of the cab driving. There was a blue plaque on Orton's old lodgings, but the plaque was set high up on the wall, out of sight. The owner didn't like to be associated with the goings-on of people like him. Orton's history included spending a stretch inside Brixton Prison for damaging library books by writing obscene blurbs on the front jackets and subtly altering the cover art.

Something to Be

What a brilliant way to waste your time, I thought. The books that Orton and Halliwell vandalised have since become the most valued items in the Islington Library Service collection. This tells you everything you need to know about the relationship between artists and the establishment. As well as defacing books, there were many episodes of cottaging to be fitted into Orton's timetable (I had been propositioned in the bogs more than once around that time: one of the inconveniences of cab driving is having to rely on public toilets), and after the cottaging there were holidays to be taken in Morocco, in the company of *Carry On* star Kenneth Williams. The purpose of these breaks was to smoke hash and have sex with elfin young boys. You might have thought that this left little time for producing work, and yet there were three novels as well as nine or ten plays by the time Orton was murdered, aged thirty-four. Unable to cope with his lover's success, Halliwell had bludgeoned him to death with a hammer.

The playwright had been only ten years older than me when he met his demise. And what had I written? One letter to the *NME* (though that had at least been published). Still, this was not a matter that unduly concerned me because I had no ambition to be a writer. I had no ambition to be anything. It was ambition with a capital A that symbolised the Blond and his crowd of mindless, upwardly-mobile, ad-exec friends, who were increasingly to be found wearing pinstripe suits and red braces and taking skiing holidays. Therefore I was against ambition; I continued to define myself in opposition to things.

The presence of *Prick up Your Ears* on the dashboard provoked a twofold knock-on effect.

One: it suggested that I might be a sexual adventurer. I was not, though there was a dangerous game that I might sometimes play with gay men when they were PoB: it was dark, I was in control, driving the car, I could be anything, and a little ambiguous suggestion never did any harm with tips. Though I found the idea of homosexual acts repulsive, I envied gay men a certain aspect of the lifestyle – if only straight girls were like them, then young men like me would be able to have sex in the toilets of nightclubs within minutes of arriving.

Two: the book suggested that I was studying drama, or English, that I was driving a minicab in the way that a pale-faced student in one of those Eric Rohmer movies would drive a minicab, to support his art. This was an idea I made more use of. With a certain kind of female, late at night, it was a notion that was worth encouraging. It could get you an invite for a glass of Merlot in a studio flat in Muswell Hill with a cheese plant in one corner and a futon on the floor. More often than not I preferred to be paid in cash, but once in a while I might clock off the plot for an hour or two.

Driving gets boring. I became restless. I had a look in on some of the north London college campuses, wondering if I ought to develop that student version of myself, the one that I encouraged fares to believe in, into a reality. But as for dole offices, the same for polytechnic and university buildings: something about the atmosphere knocked me back. The fixtures and fittings were antique, the tutors were History Men wearing ludicrous seventies moustaches. There was a better life than that on offer somewhere, surely.

Occasionally friends and acquaintances would call the cab office and ask for me by name or call number. I was a very convenient mule for the fading rock star fraternity; I was safe, so far as ferrying drugs across London late at night went. One afternoon I drove one of those fading types down to that address two doors along from Orton's old place in Noel Road.

'You wanna sort yourself out,' the rocker said, as we crawled through the traffic. 'You ought to be peaking, man, but you seem to be totally troughing.'

Rocker lingo aside, it was hard to disagree. I was invited into

Something to Be

Noel Road for tea. The place was a bombsite. A kettle was boiled on the one appliance that seemed to work, which was a brand new Aga. You can make toast on an Aga top as well as tea. The public schoolboy who owned the house demonstrated as much as he ate a bowl of cereal while burning slices of Hovis. As we began scraping the burnt bits off the toast, the rocker advised the public schoolboy, whose name was James, that I was just the man he was looking for to assist with all the building work that was in progress, or rather, wasn't in progress, on site there.

'What are you like on the end of a paintbrush?' James asked.

'He's a natural,' the rocker replied on my behalf. 'He's shit hot.'

I remembered something, which was that my dad was a painter and decorator. I mentioned this.

'It's in your blood, then,' said James. 'When can you start?'

The next day I picked up my last ever fare, PoB, and clocked off the plot for the final time, roger and out. I became, instead, a self-employed painter and decorator, the one line of work that my father had counselled me to steer clear of in the only piece of careers advice he'd ever issued.

'Look at me, son: long hours, hard work, and no money,' he'd said. 'Do something else,' he'd said. 'Do anything else.'

But once I started, I liked it. It is slow, painstaking and hard going, as the old man had stated, but nobody got on your case.

It was a matter of time and place. In the property boom of mid-eighties London, where good tradesmen were impossible to find, clients were delighted to discover that you were the kind of person who had been good enough to turn up on roughly the day you'd said you would, and had carried out the work that you'd suggested you'd do without wrecking the place. If you accomplished just that much without robbing them of their hi-fi, you were entitled to call yourself a Member of the Guild of Master Craftsmen. This sounds like an exaggeration, but it's not.

I discovered that I was naturally a rather fastidious tradesman. I added a vacuum cleaner to my tool kit, I liked to tidy up at the end of a job and leave the scene looking finished. This turned out to be enough to earn me unsolicited letters of testimonial, and gift bottles of wine and whisky. Here was the new me for the next few years: I was in business, a self-employed unit.

Meanwhile, the tenants moved out of the ground-floor flat of Toby's mother's house, and Toby and I moved in. I lived in South Hampstead now – Michael Palin was not only my neighbour, he was on the dinner party circuit that took place upstairs. At the end of my day's work I used to smoke a small joint and then go for a jog on Hampstead Heath, where I would see the recently defeated Labour Party leader Michael Foot morosely walking his dog. Bugger off and play with your friends at Claridge's, I would have thought, were it not for the fact that I had a soft spot for him, for the Aldermaston marches, for the 'donkey jacket', for the hair, for the stick, for the dog itself, for all the wonderful things about him that symbolised decent human values. Foot hadn't merely lost the general election in 1983, he had been annihilated; the Labour party manifesto was described in certain quarters as 'the longest suicide note in history'. In the months leading up to the ballot, a handful of Labour MPs had treacherously disenfranchised themselves from the party and gone off instead to drink Burgundy and form the SDP. This didn't help Foot one jot, and on top of that Maggie was feeling the benefit of the detestable Falklands Factor. O hurrah, we won a war against some gauchos on some derelict islands we'd never heard of. Labour recorded their lowest share of the vote since 1918, just over twenty-seven per cent. I felt sick on that election night, and worse the following day as I drove to work along the Euston Road, feeling that the capital city was exactly the place not to be, full as it was of cheery office clerks, secretaries and bellboys, who had all played their mindless part in the capitalist landslide.

Something to Be

With the endorsement of the landslide mandate, Thatcherism exploded into a full-blown culture of selfishness, bad taste and money-grabbing. Its energy was unstoppable, London was on fire with greed; the subject to which every conversation had to turn was the percentage rise that property prices had seen in the past week. It was a disgusting world, bereft of soul, and of human decency as represented by Michael Foot moping about on Hampstead Heath. I was opposed to absolutely everything about the whole deal, of course, but as a decorator of London homes, I was contributing my tiny part to the escalating cost of a miserable two-bed flat in Brickfield Terrace, Holloway. Or, at the very least, I was feeding off it. When I began working for James at Noel Road, I was picking up £40 a day, but as soon as I gained a level of expertise (Noel Road was a sort of finishing school where I experimented with plastering and paper-hanging, where I could fuck things up several times before getting them right), and had a few clients on my waiting list, I adopted the mantra of the building-trade pack: I 'didn't get out of bed for less than a ton a day.'

The only way I could keep my distance from the caravan of capitalist excess of which I was now a part was to distinguish myself by sticking with the second-hand Italian overcoat and accessorizing my life with other tokens of the counter-culture. The black Mini had developed a big hole in the footwell, so I sold it for a hundred quid to a ruffian from Hendon who paid me in weekly instalments of twenty pounds, several of which he missed. Meanwhile, I bought a Saab 95 station wagon, a shooting brake with eccentric 1970s Swedish body-styling, including chromed fins. It was a car that determinedly said: 'I am not a Golf Gti, I will never be a Porsche 911; I am not a yuppie.'

The pub in Noel Road is called the Island Queen. The bar featured huge papier-maché political caricatures hanging from the ceiling, including a nightmare Ronald Searle-inspired Thatcher. I would go down there for a three-pint lunch some days with the other lads from the site. James, who was at the cutting edge of telecommunications, and was the first person anyone had ever seen holding a mobile phone, occasionally joined us. The effigies would provoke heated discussion during which I would attempt to defend the dignity of labour and make the case for worker representation by trade union, while James would advocate free market economics and denounce socialism as the Work of the Devil. At the finish of one of these 'debates', James brought his ranting to a conclusion by using the expression 'I move!'

This inspired one of the lads, a carpenter, a local of Irish blood called Mickey, to break into spontaneous applause.

'It's like in the 'ouses of bleedin Parliament, innit?', Mickey said. 'Marvellous,' he continued, his eyes gleaming with unbridled admiration for an oration that would not have been out of place spewing from the mouth of a workhouse gangmaster in 1901. Mickey had voted for Thatcher. She was, 'the best thing that 'as ever 'appened to vis country'.

That Mickey was so readily impressed by a sign-off straight out of the sixth form debating society saddened my heart. He was just another working-class Tory, stepping into the booth on general election day and putting a cross against himself. Though that would not have been the way he saw it; he was motivated entirely by self-interest and was on the best dough he'd ever know in his lifetime. He had no insurance or other protection – had he cut his hand off on site, James would have given him £50 to sweeten him up and that would have represented his entire compensation package. I was in the same position myself. This was what it was like now.

The game was up: there was no going back, there was nothing collective. The motto of the south was: Look after Number One. There were millions of them. And so far as the conditions of mass unemployment up north were concerned, they were actively antithetical to people who had put themselves into that situation: Moaning northern monkeys. All the brickie from Hackney was interested in was coining it while the going was good. When James, inevitably, pulled up in a Porsche 911 one day, I was not surprised, nor was I astonished, to find Mickey and the lads walking round it with their tongues hanging out as if it were Elle Macpherson lying in the road. They circled the vehicle, stroking the bodywork and salivating, like lions looking at fresh kill.

*****

One afternoon a friend of James's turned up at Noel Road looking to borrow some welding equipment to fix the underside of a VW Scirocco. This friend was called Matthew, another of the increasingly large group that I was repeatedly bumping into, the public-school drop-out. Not that Matthew would have cleared that description for use; in his own eyes he was an entrepreneur. He was also a builder/mechanic/used-car dealer. As well as welding equipment, Matthew was looking for a decorator. James, who may have had enough of my contributions to the debating chamber, gave me the public-schoolboy reference: 'Bone idle cunt'. That was nice of him – it meant I was alright.

Amongst Matthew's portfolio of activities he had a full-time position seeing to all the small maintenance work at the new TV-am HQ in Camden Town. This station, it seems hard to believe now, originally set out to be a hard-hitting news channel, fronted by Anna Ford and Michael Parkinson amongst others. The viewing figures soon put paid to that, and the operation was taken over by the Australian media tycoon Bruce Gyngell, who got the place sorted out by diving straight down for the lowest common denominator and paving the way for Roland Rat. Also hard to believe is that Gyngell was into Buddhism and so wanted the place painted orange. This was where I came in.

Matthew's gig at TV-am came about because his sister was working there as a journalist. It was the usual London nepotism, of which I was now a part. From this moment on, I never advertised for work. TV-am journalists were buying up two-bed flats in Brickfield Terrace, Holloway, and everywhere else, like there was no tomorrow. One or two of them asked me if I did rag-rolling.

'Yes,' I said.

I asked Matthew what rag-rolling was. He didn't know either, but we found a book on it, and in no time at all I became a specialist on stippling, sponging and marbelising – all of which are 'broken-colour' paint finishes that employ archaic materials and techniques. The builders' merchants of London included in their number a small ilk of specialist suppliers where you could purchase floggers (a kind of brush) and scumble glaze (a kind of varnish). Using a flogger and some scumble glaze, you could produce a sort of waney-edged pin-stripe finish known as dragging. A good number of the journalists who worked on celebrity trivia at TV-am were gay. There were not too many things more amusing to them than the thought of employing a young man to use a flogger to produce some dragging.

And once Billie had caught on to the details of my new career, she began putting an endless supply of clients my way at ten-per-cent commission for herself.

But at the outset, for the bread and butter, I continued to 'work' at TV-am. Matthew's instructions were to proceed slowly. Sometimes I simply moved dust sheets about ostentatiously once or twice in the day, to simulate the activity of decorating; for the remainder of the shift he and I would drive out to Hertfordshire to buy a second-hand Land Rover as advertised in the pages of the *Exchange and Mart*. I would drive it back into town where he would sell it on at a profit: he was something of an expert in marking up four-by-fours. Otherwise, while we were pretending to work at TV-am, Matthew owned a property in Gloucester Road, SW5, a substantial terrace that he was converting into flats, quietly, bit by bit. He was skint, or what passed for skint in his world – down to the last ten grand of his overdraft – when we first met, but about six months later he pulled in some proper funding for the flat conversions. He reluctantly clocked off the lovely earner in breakfast television, and I joined him as his right-hand man on site in South Kensington. For the first month or so it was just the two of us. It was now that I began to listen to BBC Radio 4 for most of the day, as pop music upset Matthew's equilibrium. I learned a lot from Radio 4, regarding it as a kind of airwave-based Open University; I even tuned the station in on the radio set in the Saab shooting brake. Matthew helped by bringing me up to speed on matters about which I had no previous interest whatsoever; if he had entered himself onto *Mastermind* he could easily have selected 'The History of the Archer Family' as his specialist subject. He had the hots for Lizzie Archer. Fancying a radio character was a new idea to me, and one I liked; I thought it perverse, intriguing and not unsophisticated all at the same time.

The job was too much for the two of us, and, in need of an injection of pace on the demolition and destruction side, it was now that the Scottish ex-miners were recruited. Having Radio 4 blaring out on site was anathema to Marko and Lenny, it upset their equilibrium more than Capital Radio upset Matthew's, the sound of it practically prevented them from working. In my new role as foreman, I brokered a deal whereby Radio 1 was allowed at certain hours of the day and vice versa; we allowed Matthew to listen to *The World at One*, and, of course, to *The Archers*, which followed immediately after. *The Archers* theme tune was one that the Scotsmen soon learned to whistle.

Matthew's love life was in disarray. He was twenty-seven and already a divorcee. He occasionally went out on hopeless dates with unsuitable bindys (a word I learned meant 'dim posh girls'), and had another hopeless on-off relationship with a strange dope-smoking bohemian dressmaker who he'd met when fixing up her car. Then one night he was hit on at a party by a slightly more mature woman in his social circle. He came in very chipper the following morning, practically a new man. I met the woman and I could see why; she was like the siren in the ad for the VW Golf – sexy, haughty, chic, clad in cashmere and Agent Provocateur, no doubt, and French-looking even though she was an English Rose. She had a lot going for her, no question; I imagined she was fantastic in bed. The Scottish miners were beside themselves with envy, and it was through gritted teeth that I put on a charade of sang-froid; I really did have to force a pretence of being unmoved and unimpressed.

Matthew and the English Rose began dating. I quickly became unhappy about it because in no time at all she had him in a position I could not condone; running around like a poodle. This was because, in his view, she was out of his league. In looks, maybe, though he was no plug-ugly. He was a Tim Henman type, but a lot more convincing (if Matthew pumped his fist, you'd believe in it). So okay, he was only Henman whereas she was this year's Lancôme model, but she was not a princess – she worked for a living. She owned a fabric shop in Westbourne Grove, selling material and knick-knacks imported from Bali. She lived in a rented flat near the shop. Socially they were equals, as far as I could tell. If anything he was slightly higher up the ladder than she was.

One morning he arrived in a filthy mood. It had only been a matter of time.

'She given you the big E, mate?' said Marko, cheerfully, preparing to celebrate the moment by whistling *The Archers*.

No, she had not given him the big E. What had happened was that over dinner, at her place, they had got involved in a discussion about class. Who, or what, specifically, it was about, I don't know, but the thing she had said of someone, in a sneery way, was that they were the sort of people who 'keep a decanter on the sideboard'.

'What the fuck is that supposed to mean?' Matthew asked.

I had no idea. I had to think. My auntie Mildred might put one on display at Christmas. So I said that.

'And what does it mean when your auntie Mildred puts one on display at Christmas?' Matthew said.

'That we're going to drink sherry out of little glasses,' I replied.

'Exactly,' he said. 'That's all it fucking means, isn't it.'

'Why?' I said, 'How did *she* mean it?'

'I don't know, I kept asking her: "What does *that* mean"' he said. 'What the hell is it supposed to imply?'

'What did she say it was supposed to imply?'

'Nothing that made any sense,' he said. 'We had to drop it in the end.'

'Okay,' I said, happy that this arcane conversation was coming to a close. But I put in a follow-up question anyway.

'Why is it such a big deal?'

He went quiet; he was not going to give it away, but finally he had to explode. 'My parents have a decanter on the sideboard!' he said.

Matthew's father was a solicitor with an office in Grays Inn. I had met him once or twice. We had fixed up a few window sills at his house, a nice mews place in Islington. He was a lovely man – like John Mortimer, only a Tory.

In the years that have elapsed, I've thought about this exchange between the solicitor's son and the shopkeeper many times. What she meant to imply, of course, was that the decanter on the sideboard is an emblem, that the cut-glass vase containing Cockburn's Port or Harvey's Bristol Cream is a signifier of lower-middle-class aspirational vulgarity.

*****

Towards the latter stages of working on the current work-in-progress, my mother comes to visit me and my partner at our home in Norwich (Victorian terrace, stained-glass front door). She wants to know something about the book, and I tell her about this passage concerning Matthew and the decanter.

'We have a decanter,' she says, 'on the trolley.'

'What, that nest of trolleys with wheels at the back?'

She gives me a look. 'Yes, duck, the ones you said would be nice and handy for towing behind the car with a bag of cement on top.'

Ah yes, I did say that. How could anyone resist?

'What do you keep in the decanter?' I ask.

These days my mother spends six months of every year down in Spain in her mobile home, on a campsite, the same campsite every year, with the same people, the north-European sun-worshipping class – Germans, Swedes, Norwegians – retirees whose obsession is temperature. Their ideal is to live out their days at twenty-seven degrees in the shade; home for summer, Spain for winter. Mother is no longer with Henry, they are separated. It's brandy that she and John, husband number three, keep in the decanter, Spanish brandy, which they pick up cheap in El Supermarketo del Costa. They decant it out of the glass bottles in which it is sold in Spain into plastic gallon water bottles (to save weight, on the crossing home), and then they redecant it into the decanter on the trolley.

'It's got a ring of little glasses around it too,' she says.

'About eight of them,' says John.

Perhaps the decanter put-down, as expressed by the English Rose to Matthew in the late eighties, can no longer be made to apply in quite the same way in a world where Mother keeps a decanter full of Spanish brandy on the trolley. But though the terms of reference change, the premise of the insult is a constant.

Mother tells a tale of a woman she knows from the campsite. It is a decadent story of lust and desire; no sooner is one man dead (of a heart attack) than another man is walking around in his shoes, married to the widow. Not only is he doing that, he is living on the campsite too: he has left one woman behind in a caravan to take up with another one in a different caravan. When I say he is in dead man's shoes, I mean it metaphorically, but perhaps he *is* wearing an actual pair of dead man's loafers with golf-style tassels on his sweaty, sordid feet, because, as the story unfolds, this detail emerges: the new husband is wearing the dead man's jewellery: heavy gold chains and bracelets. He is knocking around in dead man's bling.

Mother attended the moll's wedding which took place somewhere in the region of Harrogate, the Knightsbridge of the north. It is here that the vows are traded, and it is here that Mother makes her first visit to the woman's UK winter home.

'It's a nice house, duck,' she tells me. 'All leaded windows and oak.'

What Mother means is that the house is rather upmarket and posh. The way I hear it is somewhat different. I see the property in my mind's eye. It is situated on a modern development called Riverglade where there are many similar dwellings, all built of cement-fired red bricks with herringbone pavers laid on driveways that lead to double garage doors. In the sales office the design was called 'The Tudor'. The way I hear 'leaded windows' is the way the English Rose intended 'decanter on the sideboard' to sound. The only architectural feature that I look down on more than a faux leaded window is a plastic replacement faux box sash in a Victorian terrace, a form of architectural vandalism that goes on all across the country every single day in the name of building regulations. You have to be a dedicated elitist like me to install a proper timber replacement box sash with cords and iron weights in a period home these days. The lower-middle-class bean counters who compose building regulations have rendered the matter almost impossible, because the weight of the double glazing that they insist on specifying (to save the planet from heat loss, though not from the manufacture of plastic) means that the sashes can't slide – the number of weights required to counterbalance the double glazing makes opening the window impossible: all they do is pile up all the way to the top of the cord, leaving no play for the windows to open. No doubt those who work in building regulations either already live in, or else aspire to, The Tudor, with double-glazed leaded windows.

When I was fifteen, I spent part of the school summer holidays decorating the hallway of the 1930s semi in High Lane, Stoke-on-Trent. We had panelling on the underside of the stairs, in rectangles and triangles, to follow the angle of the staircase. The panels were trimmed with a molding, like a Victorian door. I decided on a black and white colour scheme, painstakingly picking out the moldings in black. It must have looked rather Tudor by the time I had finished. I remembered this paint job, of which I was proud, as Mother told me about the moll's house. Once in a while, for a wedding or a christening, most of us find ourselves in a hotel function room decorated in the Tudor style. When this happens to me now, it's the dole office all over again; it's as much as I can do to set foot across the threshold into such an upsetting environment, and I can't get back out of the place quick enough. I have become the sort of person who feels symptoms of physical distress at the sight of decorative motifs with which I disagree.

And I have long since been the sort of person who holds toffee-nosed opinions about fenestration.

It was from Matthew that I learned box sash snobbery.

Something to Be

Matthew was a specialist at condescension, a professional holder-of-things in disdain. It was this aspect of his personality that enabled him to become so upset about the decanter on the sideboard, of course. And it was this aspect of his personality that appealed to me, because being dismissive is the required admixture that fuels snobbery. Being dismissive comes free of charge, a protective device for those who are making a fist of discarding the corporate route through life, and who, as a consequence, are usually struggling for money while elsewhere their peers are filling their boots. Dismissiveness is defensiveness wearing its suit of armour.

The Blond stopped by one day.

'So he's your friend, is he?' said Matthew after he'd gone.

'Not really,' I replied.

'Proper little office boy, isn't he?' he said, 'Nice tie. Where did you say he went to school?'

I mentioned the minor establishment; Matthew feigned never to have heard of it. Though the targets and objects of our snotty opinions varied considerably, it was the shared trait of snootiness that united us in our own uneasy friendship. Each of us had a broad range of subjects that we denigrated and despised, and a much shorter list of things we admired and revered. There was little crossover between all of this, though there was some. Matthew drove a battered green Land Rover pick-up around South Kensington and wore a battered Barbour jacket while so doing. In his view these were the only acceptable choices of vehicle and coat available to a proper Englishman, as indeed a box sash was the only acceptable kind of window.

The vehicle and the jacket each had their pro and minus points: the Land Rover averaged a mere twelve miles to the gallon, but on the other hand, no one wanted to prang their Porsche 911 on it, ergo you could float about the roads pretty much as you liked, pulling out of Kensington Gate onto Kensington

High Street without even bothering with a first glance, never mind a second. While the Barbour screamed out 'I am a Young Fogey', at the same time it also said, 'This is not a new Barbour, this is a Barbour that has been out bagging pheasants. This Barbour belongs to the gentry and this Barbour cares not a row of buttons for the whims of fashion.' The coat was host to a great many useful pockets, kept the rain out and had a detachable inner sheepskin lining for winter use – it was the acme of practicality. I abhorred it. I would have stood shivering and soaking and freezing my knackers off rather than be seen dead in it. But I liked the Land Rover. I was selectively mixing and matching, trying out the parts of Matthew that might be me. We can forget the English Rose's decanter insult that Matthew took so badly on his parents' behalf: if he'd been thinking rationally he would have told her to cart off. Matthew was upper middle class, he was certain about it, and he was almost as certain that that was the best thing to be. But his self-assurance was capable of disintegrating into self-doubt because he was permanently on guard about living up to his position. Here was something more that we had in common: he, too, tended to define himself in opposition to the expectations that appertained to people such as himself. His father would have liked to have seen him enter the offices of the law, I gathered. Though I don't think Matthew Snr made such a big deal about it, Matthew Jnr would still have felt it keenly that he had 'disappointed' these expectations. It was not class or money or background that made us similar, it was attitude. When a boy who was posher than Matthew came by one day – my friend Will, the drop-out plumber, the one who married the heir to the high street butcher's empire – I could see Matthew take against him as quickly as I had noticed it with the Blond. He was against people who weren't *just* like him. In that way we were similar too; that was why we had few friends, and why we weren't bothered about it either.

Something to Be

Because what people were there now who were just like me?

None. Back in Stoke-on-Trent my people were rolling over being complacent, letting Thatcher kill them, and doing nothing about It. They had let me down. Down here, they were southerners. I was neither fish nor fowl. I had no support network, a fact that I resented.

Matthew was a Thatcherite par excellence. The discussions we had about politics made the debates I'd had with James look like an exchange of knock-knock jokes. Our arguments were vicious, explosive and prolonged. Though we were psychologically similar, we were ideological opposites, and in the end it was this explosive combination that meant we could not work together any more. We wasted too much energy on other matters, our chemistry was too volatile. But we had lasted about a year – not bad – and though I ought, after our final huge bust-up, to have been able to find it in me to despise him, I never could. On the contrary (as he would have said). Though I never see him now, and would not consider getting back in touch, I have to acknowledge that there were elements of his style that I adopted as my own, turns of phrase that I lifted, and there was his bequest too: my love of the box sash window.

Box sash windows, though important, were not my principal fixation once Matthew and I had gone our separate ways. I was fully self-employed now, which was hairy, because I had to generate all my own business without the safety net of Matthew's regular weekly cash. I became a ducker and a diver, employing other boys on the short term, so long as the work was there, and I was doing alright. But much more importantly, I had a new girlfriend.

Marion and I had met on holiday on a Greek island, a fact and an idea that we both found amusing: a holiday romance. I had gone to Greece with the Blond and Toby. We boys were holidaying in one flat, the girls in another. Marion was a friend of the Blond's girlfriend. In the first instance this was more than enough to put me off her. Although the Blond's girlfriend originated from a nondescript area of north London (her father was a postman), she still found it in herself to look down on me, letting it be known that she regarded me as some brand of northern lowlife yob, even though I lived exactly the same lifestyle as Toby, whom she adored for being classy, like her beau. I could give her the benefit of the doubt and say that it was a personality clash, but to do that I would have had to credit her with a personality. Our feeling of antipathy was instant and mutual. So I gave her as wide a berth as possible, which was not all that wide, on a holiday. We boys returned from riding our mopeds one day to find her and Marion lying on the beach, reading. I asked them what. Where it was Jackie Collins on the one hand, Marion turned her book to show a Graham Greene cover.

'I'm on the highbrow stuff,' she said.

That comment was enough provocation to make me look at her properly. I had been blinded to her natural beauty by her taste in friends. She was petite, with beautiful blue eyes, and only the smallest parts of her firm body were covered by a leopard-skin print bikini. I sat down and started talking to her. Her choice in fiction had its natural extension in her political views; where I would have assumed the opposite (on the grounds of the company she was keeping), her politics were of the informed academic left-wing variety. I stood up, sucked my stomach in and walked around the beach kicking sand into the faces of weeds and wets, casually performed a couple of handsprings, and I bought her a Cornetto and an ouzo chaser.

Back in London, to the chagrin of the Blond's inner circle, we continued the holiday romance. Marion worked in a office near the Ritz in Piccadilly doing something bizarre. I can't remember what it was, but she was not using her gifts to the best effect; she spoke half a dozen languages, including Russian, a tongue in which she taught me to say 'I love you'.

I was taken to meet her parents, who lived in Aberdeen and Bristol respectively. They were academics and linguists, divorced; each had a new academic, linguistic partner. They each lived in tidy detached houses characterised by the absence of any sense or notion of interior design, and filled with books and files and articles. The television was only switched on in her father's house under protest. According to him, the sole reason that the set was there in the first place was so that he could watch the news from Russia (the Russian language being his speciality). It was in the pre-satellite age, but he managed it because you could pick up television signals from Finland in Aberdeen. I had never been to Scotland before, which up until this point I regarded as some part of the north of England. I came quickly to understand it was a different country where they didn't like the English. It was the same as Wales.

I was given the impression by her father that I wasn't his favourite idea of a person either, not on the grounds of petty nationalist racism, but rather because I was in some way an unsuitable candidate for the role of his only child's boyfriend. It was not that I was *socially* inferior, it was that I did not live the life of the mind. Nothing was ever said, but I could feel it, and it only added to the chip I already had on my shoulder. Over the years that Marion and I were together, which numbered fourteen in the end, and produced our son, Jack, I never met anyone in her father's circle who worked with their hands. He moved in an exclusive club, an intellectual Masonic clique consisting entirely of fellow academics. This is what academics are like. The term Ivory Tower and its connotations does, in fact, bear some translation into observable real life situations. I am sometimes invited to academic parties now that I write books: if there are ever any plumbers on the guest list, they never turn up.

I had little in common with Marion's mother either, but

she was a lovely *Guardian*-reading person who was enlightened enough to accept me as the boy her daughter loved, and that was a good enough character reference.

I was always glad to be out of both of their homes at the end of weekend visits. You could not get pissed in Bristol (in Aberdeen you could get merry, and at Hogmanay the drinking was impressive), and you could not smoke in either place. I found the atmospheres stifling, though Marion's visits to Stoke were, I think, the bigger culture shock. With Henry and Mother, smoking was compulsory, and getting pissed was more than likely, at least as far as they were concerned. Henry would usually drink enough to inspire him to rap a spoon on the table and make a speech about how we were 'always a welcome' and how the 'door was always open'. His tears would flow as his oration went on. Marion rather liked this, there was a Celtic connection, and Spanish was one of her languages too, so she could converse with him in his own tongue which secured her a place in his heart in one move. I noted there was no mention of the handicap of 'Catalunyan' not being the same language as Spanish now that an attractive young woman was involved.

Marion's slight frame and all-round delicacy marked her out as an untypical type for Stoke-on-Trent. This much was clear when I took her into the Elephant to show her off one Saturday lunchtime as a prelude to driving over to Stoke City FC to treat her to a seat (not standing) at the game. The boys in the saloon bar stood back and admired, as I had anticipated, and toned down their language, as I had also anticipated, and then showed off by playing trick shots at the pool table, using the cue-behind-the-back technique when it wasn't required, and the extravagant jump shot. So far so good, but just as we were about to leave, Dekka (Polaroid of his penis happily remaining in his wallet) still managed to make his special contribution.

'Going down Stoke, youth, did you say?'

'Yes' I replied.

'What – to the match?'

'Yes.'

'What and taking the wench with ya!?'

Dekka shook his head: it was a terrible faux pas I was committing here and no mistake.

We left the Elephant and climbed into the Saab shooting brake through the tailgate – the car had become one of those vehicles with only one way in: under these circumstances Sod's Law states that the last door working will be always be the least convenient one.

'Did he say "wench"?' Marion asked as we drove off.

'Mmmhmm,' I said.

'Is that a word round here, then?'

I had not heard it used for some time, but only because I had been absent from the city for an equivalent period.

'Mmmhmm' I said.

*****

Marion shared a large mansion flat in Putney with four other professionals. One was a teacher, one an architect, two worked in publishing. They had met in the first instance as undergraduates at Bristol University, which I came to understand was the next most elite establishment after Oxbridge. One of the flatmates had a boyfriend who worked in the building trade, at least, Will, my hero: the plumber who was even posher than Matthew. Will tortured his vowels more than anyone I'd ever heard, and by now he was competing in a big field. He didn't give a flying fuck about anything, which was one reason to admire him, and he mocked the Blond mercilessly, which was another.

'Still on the payroll? You'll never get rich like that, old boy,' he'd say.

It was an interesting jibe, and a difficult one for the Blond to deal with. The subtext was this: proper chaps are risk-taking self-employed entrepreneurs; drawing a salary is for dullards. It put Will and me into the same swashbuckling category, an alliance that enabled me to feel that I was, if not on the right lines, then perhaps not entirely on the wrong ones, in this world of professionals and upwardly mobile execs.

Will's hair was a crow's nest, his attire was filthy, his hands never clean. He drove a Citroen that doubled as a skip. He was quite often 'tight' while he was driving the skip, but he had a louche charm that allowed him to talk himself out of trouble each and every time an officer of the law pulled him over, attracted by his erratic weave down the wrong side of Putney High Road while having only one headlight working and both tail lights out. The upper classes have a different relationship with the law to the rest of us. I learned this fact by observing Will's dealings with Officer Plod; I had it cast in stone by a story I was told by a property developer called Miles, another public schoolboy who formed part of this ever-extending underworld of toff builders. Miles was a sixty-year-old ex-navy officer, ex-merchant banker and ex-fraudster: his was a victimless crime, one that practically deserved a standing ovation – he had found a way of secretly swindling a mint out of the merchant bank. But one sad day he had been rumbled and this necessitated him spending a period of time 'on holiday' at the aristocracy's nick of choice, Ford Open. He knew the beak who sent him down, he told us, they were at school together. Miles was converting a house in Wandsworth into a couple of flats. I had expanded our repertoire of activity to include the fitting of fibrous plaster cornicing: it was this work that we were doing for Miles. (Matthew and I had experimentally fitted some fancy period cornicing at Gloucester Road, an experiment that turned out well. 'I bet there's money in that,' Matthew said, as we stood back and admired our handiwork.)

Miles was an advocate of the three-pint lunch break. During one of these interludes we were talking cars. Miles told us that his father used to drive a Bentley, amongst other marques and models, and he went on to reminisce about the stories his father had told him concerning episodes that took place when his father was a young man and he and his friends were in the habit of racing their cars along Piccadilly towards Hyde Park Corner.

'This was in the days before the underpass,' he said.

'So it was just a roundabout, then?'

'Yes,' Miles said. 'When they hit the top they used to pull up the handbrake to see how many turns they could spin across the sets.'

'Sets?' I said.

'Cobbles,' he replied. 'They make an excellent skid pad, especially when wet.'

'What about the Old Bill?' I asked. 'Didn't they put a stop to it?'

Miles shook his head. 'You're on the wrong lines altogether there, young Foster,' he said. 'The Bobby used to stand at the side taking the bets.'

I pictured it, a scene straight out of P.G. Wodehouse with all the Hoorays kitted up in goggles and dinner jackets with silk scarves billowing behind them as they took part in this bally jape.

'I expect they'd had a few, too?' I said, meaning they would be well oiled.

'Well, they'd spent the night up west, but I imagine they were alright,' Miles replied.

I understood the ambivalence in this response. I had stopped over at his place once. At the end of our day's work he poured two drinks, each a triple gin with the addition of the tiniest splash of tap water, no ice. While we showered and changed he repeated that measure twice more. Nine measures of gin each, then, and after that on to dinner, detouring by the pub for two or three pints along the way, then at the bistro a bottle of wine apiece with the addition of a side order of steak and chips for the purposes of absorption. Miles drove there and back, of course (and lest we forget, there was the three-pint lunch earlier). I have never met any man who could sink so much without getting even perceptibly tight.

*****

Back at Marion's pad, bread was often broken. Impromptu dinner parties sprang up several times a week as the flatmates returned from work with comestibles picked up at Europa supermarkets that could be combined into an ad hoc menu. Here I could show off at the stove, to cover for the new absence that I had discovered in my life: I was without a Batchelor of Arts Degree. They all had at least one of these, even Will, albeit his was acquired from some dubious technical college for drop-outs. To compensate for my lack of extended formal education, I played out the role of the northern autodidact, quoting the one piece of poetry I could recite, a few lines from *Prick up Your Ears* that had somehow stuck. It was the epigraph to one of Orton's lesser-known early plays, *The Ruffian on the Stair*, which went as follows:

> *Madam life's a piece in bloom*
> *Death goes dogging everywhere:*
> *She's the tenant of the room,*
> *He's the ruffian on the stair.*

Whipping up a Sauce Anglais while reciting that stanza was my best stab at appearing to be artless and sophisticated. I could also quote John Lennon on the avant-garde: it's French for bullshit.

Though why I bothered with that I don't know, because I wasn't sure I believed it.

Sauce *Anglais* is custard made without using Bird's Instant Powder. It's best made at short order – it can curdle if left to stand – so you will be fairly half-cut by the time the requirement to perform arrives, after the hors d'oeuvre and the main courses have disappeared. Never mind, steady yourself and concentrate. Be a man about it.

Recipe for Sauce Anglais
1 pint milk
2oz castor sugar
3 or 4 egg yolks
Vanilla pod or few drops of essence

Method
Pour milk into pan and simmer with vanilla pod or essence. Light cigarette. Whip egg yolks and sugar in steel bowl. As it rises to simmering, whisk the milk into the eggs and sugar.

Return mixture to pan and place on a low heat, stirring constantly with wooden spoon until it thickens. This can take a while: about two more glasses of wine. If it looks like starting to curdle, involve the whisk; that will usually reamalgamate it.

To serve
Goes with any pudding, dessert, or afters, even ice-cream.

'Good show, Mr Steve,' said Will, the genuine upper-class article who would therefore eat absolutely anything. For him to offer comment on fodder was something, though. Will's girl, who was in publishing, and not far behind him class-wise, made

the right noises too. Will's girl could not cook to save her life.
'D'you think it's done?'
This was her catchphrase. I would frequently save her friends
from botulism by intervening in her culinary experiments, by
finishing off the cooking of a whole salmon, for instance, that she
had poached for less time than it takes to boil an egg.
'Not bad, but it's not going to pay the mortgage, is it?'
This was the Blond's response to my custard. We were about
to part ways once and for all, he and I. I had had as much as I
could stomach of his attitude to living. I could envisage its end
point even then, when we were still only in our young twenties
and I could not see far beyond tomorrow. He would end up
the stuff of a particular type of middle-class dinner party, the
kind you sometimes saw represented in a play on BBC2, one of
those excruciating occasions when a group of old 'friends' sit
around pretending to like each other, where every conversation
means something else, most of it an attack, and meanwhile the
activity that actually goes on involves the calibrating of who
has got to where in Madam Life's great journey by applying the
formula:

(equity in property - mortgage outstanding) x (other property investment [second homes]) x (pension + annuity) x
(investments) x (children's school fees + children's achieve-
ments) x (foreign holidays + timeshare) x (car) x (title
[height scaled up greasy pole in vice presidential units])
- (affairs with wives of 'friends').

Etc.

I didn't have 'a mortgage'. The Blond had to get back at Will
for his earlier comments about the payroll, and this was how he
did it, by attacking me. I was so far off the pace, so financially un-

coordinated and backward, that I was still paying *rent*, for Chrissakes. This was a situation that would not go on much longer, for a couple of specific reasons.

The first of these was the hundred per cent mortgage. You multiplied your salary by three, and they advanced you that figure. Add another, a co-mortgagee, and you could multiply it by three and a half. Here was a device that allowed you to get into the property market without having saved a penny. Saving your money in a building society or cooperative account for a rainy day was a very working-class habit, one that I did not have; no pain, no gain, let them learn the hard way and all the rest of it.

But even if you were a saver, the small change that was left out of a normal pay packet didn't mount up all that quickly, not fast enough to turn the nation into a 'property-owning democracy,' anyway. The enabling system that was put into place to speed this idea into existence involved deregulation, as it was called. It was deregulation all round. One bright spark even pushed through a piece of law that allowed for the sale of council houses. The new easy borrowing allowed the working classes a leg-up on the property ladder. This fresh supply of cheap property (like North Sea oil, it was already there: never underestimate the amount of family silver Maggie sold off) enabled a new sort of social mobility: suddenly I knew of people from Fegg Hayes who had purchased their homes under this 'right to buy' legislation. I didn't know them personally; I knew them just by using my eyes. Where the houses had previously all looked much the same, each front door painted in one of four council-approved front-door colours, the new owner-occupiers signified this fact by installing plastic leaded windows, attaching a porch and fitting a new plastic front door. Never mind the old good and bad council distinctions, here was council royalty. And what did council royalty mean, in the long term? No affordable housing for the generation that followed behind, of course.

Meanwhile, I was perfectly happy to participate in the scheme of things myself. Patrician old hands like our solicitor – Matthew's dad – were alarmed by the device that supported the hundred-per-cent mortgage: the insurance endowment policy. Matthew's father counselled caution, and his counsel was at least partially right. As they come to fruition it turns out that some of those policies don't pay off the capital amount with a tidy lump sum left over, as advertised. In fact, some of them don't even pay off the capital amount at all. That was the inbuilt design fault, ticking away like a remote device. That's the way the system falls down, right now.

The way the system fell down back then was in the slump in prices that followed the hype that the hundred-per-cent mortgages (and the associated maniac tax-allowance guillotines) generated. A new phrase entered the language – negative equity. The collapse of the property market was consistent with the cycle of boom, bust and recession that categorised those Tory years. People, rather than companies, went into 'liquidation'. First they lost their job. Then they lost their home as they sold off their asset to get the millstone of the mortgage from around their neck. Except that now it was a buyer's market, so the sale price didn't even cover the borrowing. That was negative equity; what negative equity meant was that you were homeless and twenty grand in debt too. Amusing, if it happened to yuppies, less so if it happened to yourself or people like you who now found themselves up shit creek simply because that was the only way the traffic had been directed to go.

It didn't happen to everyone, and, of course, nobody thought it would ever happen to them. On the contrary, buying property was a licence to print money, so a counsel of caution was not the kind of talk anyone was interested in. Instead, we listened to those twin armies that arrived in Burton's suits and white towelling socks: financial consultants and estate agents. You would never have touched any of these personages with a barge pole were it not for the second of the specific reasons, the one that left you with no choice *but* to buy property: rent in London was more expensive than the monthly payment on even a hundred-per-cent mortgage.

Buying a place not only equated to investing in yourself rather than keeping an absentee landlord's bank account healthy, it actually *saved* you money.

Everyone was at it. You'd bump into a couple you'd last seen six months ago out of their minds in the Dirtbox in Brixton, who you'd got talking to because of a shared northern-accent thing.

'Hey, how you doing?' you'd ask.

'Just bought a one-bed flat off Stoke Newington High Street,' they'd reply. 'Fifty-five grand.'

The flat that Marion and I jointly purchased was located in Tulse Hill, SE27, deep into that unfashionable zone where taxi drivers refuse to venture, south of the river. There have been attempts to tout the areas with access to water-frontage – Battersea, Putney, Wandsworth – as some sort of metropolitan Rive Gauche over the years, but these attempts have always failed. If I ever become rich enough to treat myself to a pied-à-terre in London, it'll be somewhere nice, which means it'll be north of the Thames. South of the river is nowhere.

Tulse Hill, a district I had never seen before, was no failed Rive Gauche. Tulse Hill was more like a cheap simulation of the Bronx, an idea I considered rather thrilling. I had found myself working on a property in Dulwich Village, which is not far from Tulse Hill in miles, though a world away in terms of residential desirability. Stopping off to look in the windows of the local estate agents, I saw a picture of this large garden flat round the back of Tulse Hill train station. It cost £40K. In Putney, it would have been £80K, in Stoke Newington £60K, in Stoke-on-Trent it wouldn't have even existed, but if it did it would have been worth about five grand.

Fictionalising the district into the Bronx at least allowed me to confer the idea of urban glamour upon an area that was otherwise devoid of a single obvious attraction. It was useful to think like this; it helped you persuade yourself into moving to somewhere you didn't really fancy, because this was *before* negative equity. This was a seller's market, gazumping was common practice and prices were escalating at such a rate that if you didn't move soon, you would miss the boat completely; in a couple of months' time even a dump like Tulse Hill would be out of your tax bracket and then what would you be looking at? The answer to that is even further away and less glamorous than Tulse Hill, the answer to that is West Norwood, where no one can hear you scream.

We moved in winter. Lots of things were missing, electricity for one, but we got it switched on just in time to get lights up on the Christmas tree. Sometimes we managed to entice friends to visit that deep, dark district for dinner, but if they were those Mancunians who had bought the place off Stoke Newington High Street, ten miles away in north London, the journey could take two hours. You could drive up the M1 to Birmingham faster.

Business was up and down, but when it was down I could at least invest in ourselves by upgrading the property, not by the addition of a porch, but by the installation of fibrous plaster cornice and the rag-rolling of the walls. Less than a year after we moved in, Marion fell pregnant.

*****

The period that preceded the birth of Jack saw the 'A Bigger Splash – Interior Design & Decorating Co.' taking on more contracts than it could handle, mainly in order to compensate for Marion's reduced earnings due to a conception date/maternity-pay cock-up situation. She missed out on it by a week or something. I was overwhelmed, and like many small building trade contractors, a bit panicky. It's this panic that explains the reason why tradesmen never turn up when they say they will. In place of turning up they spend their time drinking Maxpac coffee out of brown plastic cups under fluorescent tube lighting in the safety of a builders' merchant, or else moving materials and personnel from site to site, or else evading clients, or else sitting in lay-bys desperately employing breathing exercises designed to stave off a stress attack. Once every few months Billie would relate a story of a small-time builder or property developer who had been carried off with a nervous breakdown. Like the tales of people who found themselves in financial difficulties, it was a story that generated its own momentum: soon you heard of a crack-up every few weeks, next it was every week; once in a while you'd see someone lose it on site, a screaming fit down the phone with the bank manager would be followed by a purple-faced rush to the door and that was it – you'd never see them again.

'Awful business, darling,' Billie would say, in the aftermath of such an episode. 'Where *on earth* am I going to find someone who I can trust with a marble fireplace *now*?'

She'd look at me. No, Billie, I said. No way was I going to start experimenting with the installation of marble surrounds and the associated gas fire baskets that had become all the rage. I'd fitted the odd shower by following the instructions on the packet (they'd leaked), and bread is bread, but there were certain limits, and blowing people up was mine.

To stave off the fate of finding yourself sitting in a lay-by gibbering, we self-medicated. 'How much do you drink?' an overstretched electrician asked me one morning. We were both clearly nursing hangovers. I'd heard this question before – it often came up when you met a fellow traveller, another twenty-five-year -old with a baby on the way desperately trying to service his mortgage, overdraft and collection of credit cards.

In response to his enquiry I counter-delved: 'How much do *you* drink?'

'About four cans of Stella and a bottle of Bulgarian red,' he said. 'It's the least I need to get to sleep.'

It was the ballpark answer, that.

He told me that his old man had been out on the job with him for a couple of days not long back. Having observed his boy in action, the old man asked him the rhetorical question: 'Where's the Jag, son?'

'This lot piss it up the wall, don't they,' the electrician said to me, bitterly, as he gestured round at his collection of half-witted Cockney-Essex bellboy-style labourers.

'Piss it up the wall: *loadsamoney!*' one of them observed.

As Marion's appointment with the maternity ward neared, I was faced with similar problems. I was running out of boys to carry out the jobs, and, more importantly, to take responsibility while I was absent on 'paternity leave', of which there was none: as soon as you stop working, you stop earning. You might insure yourself against it, but nobody can afford those premiums. Being self-employed is one way of protecting yourself from having to be nice to a boss, or having to go on a 'team-building exercise' with 'colleagues', but financial insecurity is the price to be paid for freeing yourself from circumstances such as those. The statistic in common use was that the self-employed put in a sixty-hour week in order to clear slightly less than the national average wage.

And then there was the rest of the stress. I didn't have a single employee I could rely on not to fuck things up in my absence. I needed a foreman, urgently; I needed someone I could trust. I was sitting in traffic (I spent three hours a day like this) when I had a brainwave: my father was a decorator, wasn't he? Following the brainwave I considered the pros and antis. Our contact with each other remained slight, the drink at Christmas in the Conservative Club or the Labour Club (they were just two bars on opposite sides of the road, so far as anyone cared) when I was out on my errands around Stoke, and the annual phone call. It might be awkward having him around full-time, and he couldn't stay with us either, not with a new baby in a one-bed flat. I'd have to find somewhere to put him up, and that would cost. Still, at the very least, I felt certain that I could trust him not to actively rob me. And he was a time-served tradesman too, a rarity. That was more than enough on the pro side, so I called him and asked the surprise question. His life was in the doldrums, he said. A few weeks' work in London sounded just the ticket.

I picked him up at Euston Station late one evening; it was disconcerting finding my dad standing by the platform gate, looking slightly lost. I carried his bag outside to where the Saab shooting brake was double-parked. I climbed in through the back and opened up the passenger door for him from the inside. Once on the road I could see he was alarmed by the car, and more so by my driving. I didn't really have much to say to him in son-to-father terms; I felt as though we hardly knew each other. He was not an outgoing, nor a naturally articulate type. Neither am I, given the wrong circumstances, but surviving in the capital on a wing and a prayer for the previous five or six years had changed me a lot and I was able to fill space, conversation-wise ('Look – there's Marble Arch') and to give the appearance of having a sense of confidence while steering with my elbow, lighting a cigarette, diving in and out of bus lanes, running red lights, and all the rest of the techniques without which you'd never get anywhere on the roads of the capital.

The following morning, driving to the site, I talked to him about work, a straightforward, default subject that most men can manage without too much trouble. He was amazed by the contracts I had going, which were in nice properties in the better parts of Fulham. How could I be picking up work like this when I wasn't even a painter and decorator?

He asked me what I was pricing the job at. I told him, and that amazed him some more, and then I told him of the pay that I had in mind (the usual), and would that be okay? It was comfortably double the going rate in Stoke-on-Trent and was news designed to cheer him up considerably. His working technique was old school: a five-and-a-half-day week, an industrious eight-hour shift with short breaks for tea, coffee and fags, a proper job well done and a tidy-up at the close of play. In London building trade terms he was gold dust. He picked up a *Daily Mirror* and a *Sun* every day, which he read in the evenings. He was keen to locate only one other necessity of life, which was a newsagents that collected the football pools coupon. He could not miss that because if he did, that would be the week his numbers came up, guaranteed. His presence reminded me how life was lived back home. We fed him dinner at night and discovered that he would eat anything with the exception of olives. He and Marion got on fine. He looked after the contracts while I was on standby for the hospital, but sadly missed Jack's birth by having to travel back to the Midlands for a few days.

'Typical,' said Mother as she and Henry came down to wet the baby's head. 'He was in the pub when you were born too.'

Mother was just getting a dig in; all my father's contemporaries were in the pub when their children were born: that was the protocol, then. There was a new cultural construction in the air as Jack arrived – something called the New Man. New Man had been trailered through the pages of *Cosmopolitan* and had made it into the mainstream as seen in the colour supplement of the *Daily Mail*. New Man was touchy-feely and totally at one with his yin-yang feminine side. You could not *not* be a New Man in this climate, because to refuse to join in was to appear to be boorish, patriarchal and antiquated. One of the key purchases

Something to Be

I made to prepare for the advent of Jack was a velour papoose, made in Sweden, a pouch in which he could travel around south London snuggled to my chest. Babies were designer accessories, accessories that said, 'I am young, I am cool, and I am nice.' As I have already established, I am suspicious of nice people, and I have never wanted to be nice. But the baby business gave me no choice. I had been to some classes too, to do with helping your partner through labour or something. There was no choice about those classes either, and likewise your attendance in the delivery room was compulsory. Though the miracle of birth did strike me as something to see, it also struck me as something worth skipping too. It would still be a miracle, without getting a close-up of all the action.

The whole family showed up for the appearance of the first grandchild. By now, Jack's uncle Bumble had metamorphosed into a fully naturalised wigger, all the way from Tufnell Park, Kingston, Jamaica. He was living in a squat, a rundown Victorian house that was occupied by a large number of dismantled motorbikes, and which sheltered an ever-changing assortment of individuals who were always tripping, and far out. This, I disapproved of. Spliffing up after dinner parties in Fulham was one thing, weekend Charlie was one thing, but freebasing speed on a fetid mattress on the floor of a derelict house was another thing altogether. His was not some nice middle-class squat like the one Lottie had lived in, with a kitchen full of dried pulses and herbs, and Nicaraguan flags hanging out of the windows. His squat was squalid. The way the electricity was wired up constituted a danger to human life – a child could see that. People died living this way, if not through gas fumes from a botched-up boiler then from some shitty cocktail of shitty drugs. Bumble – as he later proved, by falling from the sixth floor of that block of flats and living to tell the tale – is a survivor, and he survived his squatting days. Whatever criticism I made of his lifestyle, whatever guidance I tried to give him about traditional human values (based on my own finely tuned moral code) cut no ice whatsoever, not least because he spoke a different language. He regarded the infant in his cot and then turned to me.

'Well, bludclot,' he said, 'at least you is not firin' dem blanks, innit me bredren. *Irie!*

Diane came down with Henry and Mother. My little sister was no longer so little. She seemed to think it was absurd that I was a father: in her eyes I was just a stupid big brother. She was off to university in Loughborough soon, to study to be a potter, a conceptually intact idea for someone from Stoke-on-Trent, and one I admired. Once she had left home that would be all of us out of the Potteries, a thought that saddened Mother. Couldn't at least one of us stay put, sprouting babies and getting through partners like nobody's business? Couldn't at least *one* of us be normal?

Diane would be yet another person I knew who had a BA (Hons) Degree, but she would be the first in our family.

*****

My father called to tell me of a decision he had made. This was that he was going to suspend his old life in Stoke in order to come and join 'A Bigger Splash' down in the Smoke. While this was more than useful for me – he was even happy to babysit his first grandchild (Mother: 'He never bloody babysat you!') – it was an arrangement that threw us into an odd relationship. A few weeks' help was one thing. But employment on the long term was different; several people commented that it must be curious for me having my dad on the payroll. It was, but I made the non-committal answer: it's fine. The benefits were mutual, and our relationship began to evolve into conversation too, though I had to intervene to update his lexicon, and his point of view, fairly frequently. I would be on site, consulting with the campest pair of queens in Greater London, or anywhere else, about the exact shades of peach and apricot oil-based scumble glaze varnish with which I would be marbling their bathroom walls.

'Are we working for the pouffy boys now, Stevie?' he would ask once they had gone.

'Homosexuals, father. It's perfectly normal.'

'It bloody well isn't.'

The gay element on my list were more adventurous than the average client, hence they were more lucrative. Father needed to get used to them, and to the artistic manner that I put on for their benefit, as they formed a significant part of our portfolio. We were sometimes invited to their places socially too; for the 'I've-just-had-my-flat-totally-interior-designed-and-rag-rolled' wrap party. Father donned his blazer with the handkerchief in the top pocket for these formal occasions, unconsciously fitting in rather well.

It wasn't just my clients that had the ability to perturb him. We moved in to start work in a kitchen in Chelsea for one of Billie's contacts. It was a flat that a Captain of Industry had bought on the cheap for his daughter. There had been a bit of damp coming down from the ceiling, which was badly cracked. While we had a look at that, a building contractor was investigating the outside flat roof, which had been advertised as a 'terrace'. The contractor crept down the stairs, looked in on us from the threshold and called us out.

'Come carefully, lads,' he said. 'No sudden moves.'

I asked him what was what. He took us back upstairs to show us. At a certain point in the recent past some persons had decided that the way to make a flat roof was to nail plywood boards onto the rafters and then pour a foot-thick layer of sand and cement over the top before finishing the job with a thin coat of 'tarmac' i.e. bitumen paint. This meant that the three-inch-by-two-inch timbers that were only designed to take the weight of the ceiling below were now supporting many tons of concrete. It could have caved in at any moment, and anyone standing boiling a kettle would have been flattened like a cartoon cat. The Captain of Industry hadn't bothered with a survey; now he had found out why the flat had been such a bargain.

'It has to be Irish,' the contractor said, of the roof construction.

There are many, many cowboys in a population of ten million and there were plenty more where that last one came from. We were standing on the roof of a mews house in Holland Park one morning, taking in our coffee and fags and the view. Father suddenly gestured around.

'Look at all this,' he said.

I looked. Every roof on the skyline was distinguished by the addition of a Heath Robinson outbuilding, based on a greenhouse. If these extensions were attached to anything at all it was to the chimney stack, by a few timber struts or a metal strap. The chimney stacks themselves were largely on the wonk, in urgent need of shoring-up and repointing. The al fresco garden terrace and conservatory were evidently de rigueur in W11, but a good gust of wind would surely see the streets fill up with a collection of allotment outbuildings.

'Imagine if the district surveyor down Stoke saw this,' Father said. 'It'd keep him busy for years. "*Condemned, condemned, condemned*," he'd cry. "Condemned", the lot of it.'

It was all a fabulous entertainment for Dad; this was as animated as I'd ever seen him.

So, our inversion of a more typical arrangement involving employment in the family business didn't lead to problems, not at all, at least not until the work started drying up during Thatcher's next recession. That caused me a specific difficulty, and a bad one. Though my father went out of his way to tell me not to worry, and spent the days when he had no work on being useful in the garden, the fact was that now I felt responsible for both my young family *and* my father's dwindling income, so naturally I did the sensible thing. I upped my Stella/Bulgarian red intake to danger levels.

*****

My idea of hell would be to live at the junction of Seven Sisters Road and Green Lanes adjacent to Manor House tube, north London, N4. I formed this view while I waited there for the RAC to come and tow the Saab shooting brake away after the clutch had packed up at the lights. Father and I pushed the vehicle into the curb while the traffic thundered by in six lanes and not a soul offered to help. It was raining, I was skint, every passer-by looked like a mugger or else like someone who was about to become the victim of a mugging. Grim, low blocks of thirties council flats lay in one direction, cheap hotels used by prostitutes in the other. I was only ten miles from home but it was right across town and it had taken the usual two hours to drive here through the traffic. We had been tiling a bathroom for a friend of a friend of a friend. It was an awful little job, with nothing in it, but it was the best we could get: in a recession, having your bathroom decorated to look like a Roman bathhouse is one of the first things people tend to cut back on; having basic tiling done to keep the water off the wall is a bit more essential. That was what we were down to, the essentials. As I stood leaning on the knackered motor smoking a damp cigarette, I worried about Jack and Marion at home in the flat. We had been burgled four times since we had lived in SE27, the most recent being when Jack was only a few months old. According to eyewitnesses, three youths had booted the front door down, at midday, using the technique of simultaneous kicking. Crack cocaine had arrived in the Bronx. Marion and Jack were out at the time, but my imagination ran wild over the possible scenarios had it been otherwise. It wasn't that I'd had too much of soft middle-class upbringing for this, like Midge Ure and the grape-picking. I was tough enough to deal with it, but only in theory, because nobody wants to live in fear for their baby, whatever class they're from. We had to get out.

The year before, we had met a couple on a beach holiday on Lesbos. We hit it off, exchanged contact details at the end of the holiday and then, unusually, we did something about it, driving up to visit them where they lived, in the city of Norwich in East Anglia. I had never been there before. The couple, another Marion, and a John, both taught at the university, she in social sciences, he in politics. I thought these were very cool job descriptions. As we walked around Norwich, I noted several things. I noted that the pubs were excellent, old-fashioned, stylish boozers serving bistro-like food, but that they were not completely rammed as they would be if they were located in London. I noted that the parks where Jack went to ride on the swings were clean, and distinguished by an absence of crack-heads. I also noted that the housing stock was decent, categorised by Victorian terraces, many of which retained their original sash windows. We went to an organic farm shop to buy a pumpkin that we cooked for dinner. It was bland and rather disgusting, but it was the only thing about Norwich I didn't like.

On the drive back through south London, passing by all the shops selling second-hand office furniture and passing by all the gangs of youths standing on street corners waiting to murder someone, I worried that we would arrive home to find that we had been burgled in our absence and that once more I would have to spend a night fixing locks or looking for 24-hour emergency glaziers. I put all the parts of Norwich together in my head and worked out what they added up to. They added up to an upgrade on London, so long as you regarded it in the light of that slightly abstract idea, not unrelated to the concept of the New Man: quality of life.

Part Three: Bringing it all back home

The first quality of life improvement that I noted in Norwich was how straightforward it was to get from a to b. I would never again be required to sit in stationary traffic for three hours a day, principally because Norfolk road users were apparently operating some sort of countryside code whereby the outside lane was out of bounds. This was a great help in the first minutes of getting there because I needed to put my foot down and move with a sense of urgency, as we had been considerably delayed in leaving Tulse Hill by our cat, Sandro (after Botticelli – it was Marion who had had named him; I didn't know who Sandro Botticelli was). Sandro had escaped through his cat flap in the last minutes before the removal men set off in their van. Sandro was spooked and refused to return to us, and eventually we *had* to leave, and he had to be left behind, which made for a tearful journey to our new home on Marion's part.

The removal men were a cheap and cheerful outfit from Peckham.

'Looks quiet up here,' one of them said.

'Nice place to bring up kids,' another said.

'Quiet,' said the third. 'Listen! – you can't hear a thing.'

They got into a chorus: Quiet, hmm, nice and quiet. Quiet. Nice. Nice and quiet.

My interpretation of all this banter was that they weren't entirely convinced about the wisdom of our move, away from the happy bustle of SE27. The quiet unnerved them, I could tell. Most of their work took place within Greater London and the Home Counties and I formed the impression that they wouldn't feel totally comfortable until they were back within the M25, when things would get a bit noisier and everything wouldn't be quite so quiet.

I knew what they meant. When they had gone, Marion and I sat in the front room of the modest, rundown Victorian terrace, with all its original features intact, and looked at each other. It was like the scene with Robert Redford at the end of *The Candidate*: what the hell do we do now?

Early on the first Sunday morning, I took Jack to the local park. The children's playground was in a beautiful setting with a hundred-year-old oak tree overhanging the play equipment. There was no one else there. At the other end of the park two elderly men wearing whites knocked up at tennis, on one of ten grass courts that were available for hire at two quid an hour. The only grass courts I'd seen before were at Queen's Club in Barons Court, facilities that were not open to members of the general public, facilities that only came for a substantial annual membership fee. I could take up tennis again; I hadn't played for years. It was nice. It was quiet. It was nice and quiet.

I had never once considered moving back home, that is to Stoke-on-Trent, which was where I said I came from, when people in Norwich asked. I did not, of course, say that I came from London: I was not a Cockney-Essex bellboy. I still regarded my birthplace as myself, we were one inseparable concept, albeit that I continued to think of the city as a doomed anachronism. I imagined describing the concept of rag-rolling to Dekka. I imagined his response, once he had absorbed the idea and stopped laughing: wenches' work.

The area we moved into in Norwich is known as the Golden Triangle, which is an estate agents' expression. The thing that is golden about the triangle is its property prices. The streets are a mile or so from the University of East Anglia campus, and consequently they are the streets in which many of the tutors live. The houses come in several grades, from the smallest straight-in-off-the-pavement terraces for junior lecturers to the house on the hill where the dean of studies may reside. The vice chancellor lives in a mansion in a village five miles south, the actual chancellor has his own helicopter landing pad, and in all likelihood a palace to go with it. The streets of the Golden Triangle constitute a middle-class enclave, containing the bistro pubs where the tutors eat and drink, and the parade of shops on the main road where the delicatessen stocks eighteen different kinds of organic Cheddar a few doors along from a proper wine merchant. The wine merchant has since closed: it has become instead a combined art gallery and shop, a shop of the type where you can decorate and glaze your own crockery with your child's handprints. Further down the road there is a children's clothes shop where OshKosh B'Gosh and Pommes Framboise designer wear is traded and exchanged.

When we arrived in 1989, one in every three cars displayed a Greenpeace or a 'Nuclear Power – *Nein, Danke!*' bumper sticker; one in every three people wore clothes made out of hemp. Our next-door neighbour on one side played a saxophone very well, if rather too frequently, and had a plaque on his wall advertising the day job: Acupuncture Clinic. Next door on the other side they were Buddhists, well into yoga. This was where I lived now. It was neither the north nor the south: it was the east, but if you drew the line and only had two choices, it was the south. Some kind, well-meaning people invited us for dinner where they served a huge bowl of vegetable stew and another huge bowl of couscous with courgettes in it. This was what I ate now, if I wasn't careful.

I ought to have liked it, I ought to have felt at home, being sur-rounded by the liberal intelligentsia and left wing do-gooders. But I was not entirely comfortable. The quietness I could deal with, the niceness I found irritating. But I preferred the scene to Tulse Hill – I could at least say that.

The university campus is notable for its brutal, modernist sixties concrete architecture. When I felt overwhelmed by the niceness of the streets in which we lived and by the kindness of our neighbours, I would take Jack up there. It was an ad-venture playground for a small child: the ramps and walkways that run between the ziggurats and the famous teaching wall – a long sheet of glass and concrete – work perfectly as a hide-n-seek arena. I particularly liked it if it was raining; this was what it must be like in the Eastern Bloc, I thought. I would put on the Italian overcoat and pretend to be in Poland. And also, it reminded me of home: if Stoke-on-Trent had architectural form, it would be the UEA. There were very few people about at the weekends; I would carry Jack on my shoulders, looking into the empty class-rooms, wondering if I would like to study there myself. Maybe. But study what? And live on what, too? Marion doted on Jack; it seemed harsh to force her back to work. And anyway, they're not young for long. It's better that their mum looks after them than a nanny. Nannies are middle class and wrong, they are an excuse for proper parenting. These, I believed, were my own thoughts. I might have been hemmed in on all sides by the alternative life-style brigade, and have someone from Amnesty International knocking on my door every second day looking for a signature on a petition, but I still had principles and I was *not* middle class, even if people who came to visit (from Stoke) thought otherwise, with me living as I was amongst people who talked about ideas in posh voices. I couldn't possibly be middle class when I spent my Saturday afternoons and sometimes my Sunday mornings still at work, applying gloss paint to skirting boards – always the final act of finishing off – a knee- and back-breaking activity that I was doing far too much now that I was all but a sole trader. The best thing I could say about painting and decorating at the ordinary, basic level of rubbing down and undercoating was that it gave me plenty of time to think.

*****

If you looked at the map of the country on general election night, Norfolk would be all blue with just the single red dot in the middle. There is a city/county divide in East Anglia, and the red dot is Norwich. One winter's day a big party broke out in the dot. Margaret Thatcher was deposed, joy was unconfined: the wine merchant in the Golden Triangle ran out of champagne. The elation was short-lived, though; John Major simply took over where Hilda had left off. I survived his first recession by the skin of my teeth, but not his second.

It wasn't only me. Everyone went to the wall. I could have blamed Major, I suppose, but actually I blamed myself. I had heard of something called the 'poor boy's fear of success', and I wondered if I had that. Was it easier to fail, to remain in a comfort zone where you took no responsibility for things that happened to you, where you blamed your life on the outside forces of politics and circumstance? No, it was not easy to fail, it was hard. I was back in rented accommodation, my young family was in rented accommodation. It hurt.

Meanwhile my sister graduated from Loughborough art school. I don't think I knew anybody now who didn't have a degree, with the exception of Bumble. We went over to see Diane's degree show. She had made a collection of Etruscan-style pots with volcanic glazes dripping down them. They were beautiful, and she gave me one for a present. I walked around the art school, which smelled of oil-paint and turpentine, of clay and of solder. The scent was akin to that of a building site. The efforts of the students amounted to something more than a freshly decorated dining room though, of that I was sure. Back in Norwich I signed up to an A level night course in art where I learned who Sandro Botticelli was. Sandro the cat had meanwhile gone feral; he was a homeless animal who had taken to living in the garden back in Tulse Hill. One day the new owners of our old flat drugged a plate of food and left it outdoors. He made the journey back to us under anaesthetic, in a cardboard box in the guard's van of the train.

A year or two after starting the A level, I was accepted into Norwich School of Art and Design. After seeing Diane's degree show, I had stuck my head into this institution a few times. Unlike the dole offices and the polytechnic campuses of north London, I found that I could pass the threshold quite easily. It was the smell, again. I was at home with it. I liked the building too, an old Victorian technical institute in the middle of the city, distinguished by even lines of long box sash windows on every floor. I had gone down there to try to enrol on a foundation course. I was too late, they were already full; maybe next year. The man who interviewed me turned the subject to literature. I can't remember how. I told him what I was reading: *In Cold Blood*, by Truman Capote. He picked up his internal phone and got me a second interview with something called Cultural Studies. They teach and study writing there, he said, Maybe they would take you on. And they did. Like practically everything else about my 'career' to date, it was pure accident that I was accepted onto the course that would change my life. But going down to the art school in the first place had been a decision, the first move I had made on my own behalf for a long time that was not reactive. It was not since I'd gone to catering school that I had defined myself in favour of something, rather than against it. I was *for* an education.

Bringing It All Back Home

The BA (Hons) in Cultural Studies was a new degree, one that entailed spending your time in three equal parts: in the study of art and social history, in the making of visual images, and in creative writing. The course title was one to inspire mockery. Was it the new Media Studies? What did we do all day, sit about watching old episodes of *The Sweeney* (yes, you could do that) and writing dissertations about Madonna's bra (yes, you could do that too, but you'd have to read, absorb, and apply post-structural feminist theory to get a decent mark for it). But I couldn't care less what people said about my course; in fact, I liked it. The other departments of the school were against us CS students too, we were new-fangled and, in their view, we stole space from them. I had rejoined mainstream education and yet I was still able to feel myself part of a repressed minority. Nothing could be more ideal. I sat on the floor of a classroom at the top of the school one afternoon and watched the sun stream in through those sash windows. The tutor, and poet, George Szirtes, circulated photocopies of the poem 'Home Burial' by the American laureate Robert Frost. I had never heard of either poem or poet, though some of my fellow students had and enthusiastically shared their opinions. I felt slightly awkward, as disorientated as Sandro the cat when he got off the train, and somewhat behind, but I loved being there. I felt lucky to be spending my days like this. I was in the last cohort of students to receive a grant rather than a loan. Four grand a year went into my bank account: if I worked most weekends and all the holidays, we could survive. Marion was back at work. Because art school hours are flexible I could look after the childcare, an inversion of normal circumstances, or not, if you opened your eyes and looked around. Students managed their time in ways that allowed them to do the most important thing in their lives: be at school. The time and motion of the school run, love affairs, part-time jobs, essay deadlines, and all the rest were manipulated to ensure as much. Was it a very middle-class world, as some imagined, full of Rich Kids indulging in a little daubing? No. I never, ever thought of it like that. A good number of students were mature, or had worked for a few years before landing here. It was these categories who tended to get the most from their degree – by using the facilities as much as possible and only spending relatively short sessions in the bar – because it was these categories who knew what the alternatives were out there in 'the real world'. I was thirty-two now; if I had gone to art school at eighteen I would very seldom have made it to a seminar. But I was no longer eighteen and I was always in class. It was during one of these seminars that a tutor used the expression 'cultural capital'. Money still held no interest for me; I regarded it like the weather: it was always there, and it changed, but it was only a part of life, it was not all of it. Art and ideas were another story, much more important than the weather. If I could graduate and turn either of those subjects into my work, make them into what I did, perhaps I, too, could produce cultural capital. This, at last, was something I thought worthwhile. Here, finally, was a commodity I could commit myself to.

I was not, as it turned out, all that much of a visual artist. At a certain point I responded to a brief called 'A Sense of Place' by writing a story called 'Swimming'. I had recently visited my mum in Stoke and had driven past my old Victorian middle school which had been knocked down. That prompted me to drive to my old Victorian swimming pool, which was still there, though the absent school made me wonder for how much longer. My story consisted of a sort of dialogue between my old world and my new self. I looked at Stoke differently now; through the eyes of someone who was immersed in social history, critical theory, visual representation and creative writing. I looked at its people, its geography and its history and I considered them to be my people, my geography and my history. I could not see much of this represented anywhere in culture, so for my final degree show piece I wrote a book of short stories set in the city. I accompanied each story with a front-plate colour sample from a decorator's chart. That collection was called *Close Quarters* and was published a year later under the title *It Cracks Like Breaking Skin* by Faber, T.S. Eliot's old firm. If I never did anything else, that was good enough for me. You could get the book out of the library. It had an International Standard Book Number. It had cultural capital.

In the May of the year I graduated, New Labour came to power in a landslide. I sat up in bed all night slowly getting through a bottle of Fleurie as I watched the coverage. Prior to the count it had looked as though it would be a close call, which meant that Labour would lose, again. I had learned many new words at art school, one of which was *jouissance*, a French term meaning something like 'a blissful carnival of pleasure'. The Tories had been in power for the whole of my adult life; and now, finally, they were not. I never thought I'd see this day. The following morning it was *jouissance*, *jouissance* everywhere. The red dot of Norwich had drunk itself sober and had a hangover to savour.

The *jouissance* didn't last all that long. You'd wish it were otherwise, of course, but the New Labour breed of Mandelson-inspired academic apparatchik have done their best to destroy the Norwich School of Art and Design over the years that New Labour has been in power. All the actual artists on the teaching staff, remnants of the sixties, the ones who inspired us, were forced out, and management structures were put in their place. It's a familiar and depressing story. One day a memo went round via email informing employees that all forms were to be filled in using one specific font, and one specific point size. The principal no longer resides in the Victorian technical institute where the students learn, as used to be the case, but instead pulls the strings from a bloc of 1950s offices around the corner, a building that reminds me of the dole office in Stoke-on-Trent, circa '78. It's not even called an art school any more. They may not be Tories, and there's no other realistic way to vote, but New Labour and its manifestations has never given working-class heroes all that much to cheer about.

After the short stories I wrote a novel, and then a set of extraordinary circumstances involving goings-on at Stoke City FC meant that I persuaded my agent to persuade a publisher that you could sell a book about that wretched team. Stoke City FC had been stylish, heroic and successful when I was a young teenager, but they had been underperforming for twenty years since then, and were in some sense a metaphor for what had happened to the area. In the same way that I always said, if asked, that I came from Stoke, the answer to which football team I supported came even quicker. I had kept an eye on Stoke City over the years, and had turned up on the terraces now and then when they were in the vicinity. Late on in the year 2000, I took Jack over to the Midlands to a night match, a cup-tie, for a treat. We lost eight-nil to Liverpool. It was this epic reverse, and the black humour that you could hear in the crowd as the goals went in against us (at nil-six: 'C'mon Stoke, we can win this!') that convinced Jack, who was twelve now, that Stoke were the team for him. The football book takes the form of a season-in-the-life-of account. This meant that Jack and I travelled to Stoke and back once a fortnight, and that we sat or stood on an away terrace alongside the same few hundred diehards – those who devote their time and income to watching the team home and away – on the alternate weekends. This put me back amongst my own people every week for the first time in two decades. I was from the same stock, of that there was no doubt, but I was no longer *of* them, nor had I been for many years. On our long miles on the road, Jack played his hip-hop compilations. Occasionally I'd get fed up of the rap, pull rank, and inflict my own music on him. Paul Weller had long since gone solo, personal and bucolic. He wasn't my son's cup of tea at all, though he quite liked the track 'Wild Wood' from the album of the same name. Not for these lyrics:

Knowing, just where you're blowing
Getting to where you should be going

but for some inchoate whooping noises in the middle of the song.

I had stopped relying on Weller's lyrical advice some time ago, but I am pleased to see that he has turned out to be the one punk/mod revivalist to have managed a full, mature and extended career. Over the years I had met many people who did not care for Weller or his sound, those who found his overly-defined, chippy Englishness 'daggy', But he has proved much more durable than most. The working-class boy from Woking, who I once hero-worshipped, no doubt owns a mansion near Godalming in Surrey these days. If he does, I don't hold it against him. I have changed.

Occasionally, especially at away fixtures in London, I would spot another like me, dressed a bit too smartly, driving away from the game in a German car, using the occasion to reignite something of himself. Over the course of that season-in-the-life-of I made new friends: one, Elt, the marketing firm owner with whom I shared the raspberry beer and schnapps chasers, another his brother, Lee, who mocked us for that, and for a lot of other things too. Lee describes himself as 'a proper working-class bloke, not a gayer like you pair'. In the style of a good host at a party, it was a proper working-class bloke – a pensioner, ex-miner and eccentric – who put Elt and me in touch with each other in the first place.

'You two will like each other, you've both betrayed your roots,' he said with a twinkle in his eye.

We knew he meant it, but we also knew that he might find it

in his heart to forgive us, since we could still be bothered to support our hometown team. And we did our bit to help him along too, as, during the course of the interminable, awful games of football, we diverted him by talking about the merits of Sancerre and grower's bottles of Champagne, the escalating cost of Barolo, and about whether it was better to make bread and butter pudding using Hovis and currants, or brioche, marmalade and vanilla sugar.

Following Stoke City is the opposite of backing a winner. At the point of bringing this manuscript to a close they had been out of the top flight for twenty-three years, the second half my life. They were the only Midlands club who bear their city's name never to have played in the Premiership. I was certainly as pissed off as my fellow fans about the abject side and its dismal manager; that, at least, united us. I was used to failure; that I think united us too, even if, by now, I was a success.

But being a writer is a compromised sort of success. It looks good, and I know that both of my parents and Henry are proud to say what it is that a Stephens does for a living. Even Bumble has been known to pay respec'.

'Your books is plenty boring, man, innit, but you as done well, me budclot. *Irie!*'

I don't think any writer can ever feel comfortable, though: there's not much in the way of job security, and in that sense, at least, *plus ça change*. Norman Mailer said that writing is the exact opposite of capitalism, that the way you live is with the expectation of disappointment, rather than the expectation of more success; the harder you graft, the more you learn your trade. If by this he means that you expect each new publication to bomb, he's right.

But it's not all bad. In writing you've finally found an occupation that suits your disposition, in which it's desirable to live in several places at once: one foot in the culture of here and now, one foot in the culture of there and then. It helps your work to be like this. The more you know about, the more material you can call on. It's not so much that social mobility is desirable in writing, it's that it goes with the turf.

*****

After the final parent dies in many of the genuine middle-class cases, there is the family home – a million-pound semi – which was purchased for £20,000 in 1953, located somewhere in the Home Counties, to dispose of. Once the conveyancing has finally taken place, there is a tidy sum to be split between two or three offspring. Here is the injection of capital that allows the middle classes to shell out more on the doing-up of a kitchen than their family seat cost in the first place, with change left over for the second home in the Languedoc, and maybe even a third in up-and-coming Morocco. They are *always* sniffing out the new real estate hotspot; nothing is more important to them than property location.

This is how I am middle class: I always study the property pages in *Tatler* when I'm at the dentist.

This is how I'm not middle class: I'll never see the injection of capital from the sale of the house in Guildford that will enable me to act on the *Tatler* advert and buy the modernist beach hut in Lausanne for half a million Euros.

I am always chasing money; in that way, at least, I am still as working class as the next one.

Chasing money takes me to odd places. I am at a literary party. At one level, I am amongst fellow travellers, comrades, but at a much more honest level, I am simply surrounded by irritating rivals who keep writing *other* books, some of which might even be good, who compete against me in the Darwinian struggle for shelf space in bookshops and supermarkets. The main thing that writers have in common is that they don't like each other. Many are privately educated, many are Oxbridge. Those working-class scribes who make it through to publication are in the minority, and we don't like each other either. Larkin said he preferred not to do readings because he didn't like to go about the country pretending to be Philip Larkin. Perhaps he avoided literary parties too. The moment is never long coming at these events when this thought crosses my mind: 'Who are these people; what *am I doing* here?'

It is the moment when I can no longer be bothered to pretend to be Stephen Foster.

George Orwell describes my situation in *Wigan Pier*. One of the things that I admire about Orwell is that everything makes him angry. One of the many things that riled the Old Etonian was people like me, plebs done good in the highbrow world of literary darlings. Here he is, summing us up:

> ...it is a pity, though it is a natural result of the scholarship system, that the proletariat should tend to interpenetrate the middle class via the literary intelligentsia. For it is not easy to crash your way into the literary intelligentsia if you happen to be a decent human being.

O dear.

> The modern English literary world, at any rate the highbrow section of it, is a sort of poisonous jungle where only weeds can flourish. It is just possible to be a literary gent and to keep your decency if you are a definitely *popular* writer – a writer of detective stories for instance; but to be a highbrow, with a footing in the snootier magazines, means delivering yourself over to horrible campaigns of wire-pulling and backstairs-crawling. In the highbrow world you 'get on', if you 'get

on' at all, not so much by your literary ability as by being the life and soul of cocktail parties...

I can say 'book' and 'bath' for you if you like, George.

> ...and kissing the bums of verminous little lions. This, then, is the world that most readily opens the doors to the proletarian who is climbing... Many of them are very disagreeable people, quite unrepresentative of their class, and it is most unfortunate that when a person of bourgeois origin does succeed in meeting a proletarian face to face on equal terms, this is the type he most commonly meets.

O dear, *encore.*

George goes on to explain that what I am about to do to that poor bourgeois individual is to borrow a fiver off him, a fiver that he will never see again. Not true: I once had to touch a publisher for a sub for a taxi, but I sent it back by return of post the following day.

Fortunately, I don't really care what Orwell thinks. I admire his writing, because it's brilliant. That's enough for me. The world has changed since *Wigan Pier;* there are no miners here any more. It has changed, and also it has stayed the same. There remain pockets where social codes are just as Orwell describes them above. I have given a reading once or twice and seen the matrons of Brighton squinting at me: how has such an uncouth example managed to make it *into the public domain*? I have given a reading in Stoke too, at the reopening of the newly refurbished Town Hall. I was asked to perform next to a Punch and Judy stall *while the show was actually on.* Best stick to Larkin's modus operandi and not go around pretending to be yourself. Best stay at home. At least that way you will avoid finding yourself in the situation that always arises at a literary do when a waiter offers you a husk of ciabatta and a bowl of olive oil to dip it into. Not all middle-class comestibles are acceptable.

Q. What is the recipe for ciabatta?
A. Make dough, mould into the shape of a shoe. Leave out in the sun until holes develop and it goes hard.

You find yourself back home some time after midnight making a plate of 'Cheese' and rather wishing you had a couple of slices of Mother's Pride to mop it up with.

*****

I am in the branch of Waitrose in the suburb of Norwich, the one where I had the conversation with the dean of studies about buying space.

Behind me I hear a child say this: 'Mummy, it's my turn to do the brassica this week.'

These are the words of a child who will certainly not scream at the sight of an aubergine. There is a note of excitement in the voice, a note that strikes me as inconsistent with a vegetable. I am facing the other way. I am considering whether I can, in all good conscience, purchase a bag of mixed lettuce leaves. It's not that I am feeling morally compromised about the working conditions of the immigrant labourers who are used to pick and wash the rocket and the chard. I know this is how the leaves get here, into the bag in Waitrose, because I have seen the immigrant labourers standing about on street corners in the early morning, smoking, waiting for the minibus to pick them up and take them to work. Some nights in November I have seen them picking beets in fields under arc lights as I have been driving my dogs back from a late walk on the beach. The local newspaper tells me that they will have to hand over all their earnings, bar three quid, to criminal gangmasters. But I'm not worried about them, they're not my problem, I don't really care, to be honest. Liberal hand-wringing just isn't my thing, it makes me squirm. I could never bring myself to buy Naomi Klein's cult book, *No Logo*, for instance, not only because it was so boring, but because it practically glowed with sanctimonious hand-wringing. Plus which, it sold well, much better than the book that I had out at the time. Plus which, boycotting *No Logo* allowed me to indulge my preferred racial prejudice: I'm anti-Canadian (because they're so boring). So no, it isn't that I care about the living conditions of Polish immigrants, it's that I regard the acquisition of bagged-up lettuce as incorrect behaviour *for a chef*. The problem that has been created by combining leaves like this is one of excess choice; you'd have to buy five vegetables and three kinds of herbs to get the medley of flavours on offer for £1.49. Which would lead to waste. Even if you made lettuce soup with what was left over, you'd end up throwing some of that away, because lettuce soup isn't all that great. So I pick up a pack of plain rocket instead, a possible alternative.

The child says her line again, more excitedly.

I'm compelled to turn, to see what exactly it is that's so fabulous. The voice belongs to a young girl, one of three or four young children who, together with their preternaturally fresh-faced mother, look as though they've stepped directly out of an ad shoot for low-cholesterol olive oil spread. The child is weighing the vegetable. That is all. That is what it was her turn to do. There's nothing wrong with weighing vegetables, but nonetheless, something about the tableau nauseates me. I have seen worse; I saw a three-year-old girl, wearing hand-knitted striped socks and a Buddhist hat, whirling around an organic greengrocers, dancing to the ethnic music they were playing – which was by world music darling Manu Chao (and I could identify that) – early one morning *during the same week*. Her mother smiled on indulgently, as if this was the greatest thing ever seen, as did all the other hippy shoppers.

As I drive home from Waitrose, I begin to work out why I'm so hacked off. I remember hearing a report on Radio 4 some while back, from Glasgow. A government agency had gone into the tenements there in an effort to improve the diet of the local children, because cases of scurvy had been reported. The government people had been shocked to find that, upon being offered bananas, some of the children tried to eat them without peeling them. It's a story that forces you to wind back a few frames to think it through: not only had those children never encountered a banana before, they had never, in any situation, not in a film or on television or in a picture book, seen anybody eat one. Not even a monkey. They had never been taken to a zoo.

I'm on the side of those children, not the brassica-weighing poppet who knows the Latin for broccoli, though I do not want to live in a tenement in Glasgow. I am content to be in Norwich.

The car I drive home in is a ten-year-old Volvo estate. I bought it in a moment of opportunity, because it was cheap. 'You were ripped off,' my Stoke boys advised me, laughing in my face when I mentioned the bargain price that I paid. I bought it from my friend the professor of politics with whom I play a weekly game of squash (I have given up smoking to such an extent that I now put filters into the roll-ups). The Volvo replaced a fifteen-year-old Mercedes estate, a car the younger of our two dogs had put beyond economic MOT repair by eating all the seat belts in the back. I absolutely hate the Volvo, I cannot live with it, for this specific reason: it allows people to identify me as something I am not, it allows them to imagine that I'm a genuine member of the middle classes. As soon as I have finished this manuscript I am going to replace it with a different vehicle, which will be a ten-year-old Mercedes estate, a car that I regard as déclassé. A ten-year-old Mercedes estate is as likely to have an Indian cab driver behind the wheel as it is the 2nd duke of Manchester. Déclassé is the condition I aspire to. I am middle class enough to count that as my ambition, which is no ambition at all. A déclassé hero is something to be.

Also by Stephen Foster:

The *Sunday Times* bestseller

Along Came Dylan
Two's a crowd when you've been top dog

£7.99   paperback

Ollie was just about cured of his basketcase habits: the neurotic lurcher at last appeared to have his paws planted firmly on the ground (well, almost.)

But did Stephen Foster take a well-earned rest? No. He decided one thing was missing from Ollie's life, someone who could really understand him, a friend with whom he could have dog-to-dog chats.

"If you must get another dog, get a girl," the experts told Foster. So he has got a boy, a pure-bred Saluki lunatic called Dylan. As soon as the new puppy peered through the door, Ollie threw his master a look of contemptous disbelief that said, "I refuse to have anything whatsoever to do with this. You're on your own, pal."

The riotously funny *Along Came Dylan* takes up where Foster's bestselling *Walking Ollie* left off, but instead of one canine conundrum, now he's got two: Dylan, the outlaw, proves to be virtually untrainable; Ollie, feeling threatened, becomes increasingly antisocial, and Foster is caught in the middle wondering why man's best friends can't just be friends.

A holiday snap of Stephen in the eighties

Stephen Foster is the author of the short story collection
It Cracks Like Breaking Skin, and the novels *Strides* and *Are You
With Me? She Stood There Laughing*, his story of a season follow-
ing Stoke City, was one of the bestselling sports books of 2004.
Walking Ollie, the account of his early days with his rescue
lurcher, Ollie and the sequel *Along Came Dylan*, were both
Sunday Times bestsellers. He is the Royal Literary Fund
Writing Fellow at the University of East Anglia.
He lives in Norwich with his partner, Trezza.

Note: Stoke City eventually regained their rightful place in
the top flight. Stephen Foster will chronicle their Premiership
journey in *And She Laughed No More*, Short Books,
Autumn 2009.

Special thanks to Vanessa Webb, Ben Keane and Sith